Self Hypnosis for Cosmic Consciousness

Achieving Altered States, Mystical Experiences, and Spiritual Enlightenment

Ronald A. Havens, PhD

Crown House Publishing Limited
www.crownhouse.co.uk
www.chpus.com

First published by

Crown House Publishing Ltd
Crown Buildings, Bancyfelin, Carmarthen, Wales, SA33 5ND, UK
www.crownhouse.co.uk

and

Crown House Publishing Company LLC
6 Trowbridge Drive, Suite 5, Bethel, CT 06801-2858, USA
www.CHPUS.com

British Library Cataloguing-in-Publication Data
A catalogue entry for this book is available
from the British Library.

10-digit ISBN 1904424546
13-digit ISBN 978-1904424543

LCCN 2006934877

Printed and bound in the UK by
Cromwell Press, Trowbridge, Wiltshire

"The spiritual implications of hypnosis grow out of man's deepest need, that of wholeness, of At-one-ment, of the re-uniting of all that is separated which belongs together."

Bertha Rodger, MD (1965)
in
Religion and Hypnosis Meet

Contents

Acknowlegments

I must begin by gratefully acknowledging the inspiration of Bertha Rodger, MD. She introduced me to the possibility of hypnotic transcendence and started me down this path. The wisdom and artistry of Milton H. Erickson, MD, provided the tools required to negotiate this path, as did the insights and support of his many students, friends, and relatives. My deepest thanks to them all. I also wish to thank my own students, clients, friends, and relatives for listening to my many harebrained ideas over the years and for offering their input to this final product. None of them, however, has been more patient or encouraging than my wife, Marie. She deserves a special award, and I will see that she gets it.

Finally, I would like to thank the editors and staff of Crown House Publishing. They are friendly, competent, tolerant, ethical, and honest. Who could ask for anything more?

Preface

This book contains straightforward instructions for creating spiritual, religious, or mystical experiences within yourself and others. It offers detailed descriptions of these transformational epiphanies, as well as potential explanations for their short and long-term healing effects. More importantly, perhaps, it provides verbatim examples of hypnotic procedures that were specifically designed to precipitate such life-changing events.

Whether enlightenment experiences are purposefully induced or occur spontaneously and unexpectedly, these altered states of mind and body invariably confront us with the oneness, timelessness, beauty, truth, and perfection of ourselves and of the universe. They offer an unbiased and expansive view of the world that challenges and replaces our limited way of knowing and perceiving. As such, they reintroduce us to the awe, wonder, and joy of childhood while surprising us with the passionate spirituality and sensuality of adulthood. They connect us to each other and fill us with a deep appreciation for the fundamental forces of nature. Ultimately, they convey an essential but inexpressible truth, a truth hidden deep within us all that removes our anxieties, tensions, and pains, soothes our angers, calms our bodies, and leaves us with a feeling of freedom, contentment, and inner peace.

It is likely that every normal human brain has the inherent potential to experience the world from this integrative and self healing point of view. We certainly seem to have the desire and the tendency to do so when given an opportunity. Perhaps that is how we experienced the world at birth, as completely unified, perfect, and wholesomely accepting. That would explain why so many of us yearn for that experience as adults. Perhaps we are drawn to such a state simply because every sexual orgasm we have offers us a brief glimpse of what it would be like to truly transcend the fetters that bind us to the tides and times of earth. We would be able to relax and merge completely with each other and with the pleasure of it all. Whatever the reason, such states of mind and spirit do appear to be universally recognized and sought after. Every culture throughout history has a name for this unusual and powerful experience.

Unfortunately, from my perspective at least, every culture (and every cult) has also evolved rather complex and demanding techniques for attaining this ecstatic state of mind. Some require years of commitment to meditation and the study of detailed descriptions of alternate realities. Others demand a total withdrawal from ordinary life and require followers to enter into the seclusion of a monastery, to wear a specific costume, and to participate in repetitive rituals. A few use psychedelic drugs to attain the desired state and, recently at least, many groups, gurus, and spiritual leaders have begun charging rather exorbitant fees to join their "special" journey toward nirvana.

Whenever I give talks on this topic to groups of mental health professionals, I always ask if anyone has ever had the kind of experience I am describing. Invariably, over 90% raise their hands. Furthermore, the relevant literature is full of examples of ordinary people suddenly becoming immersed in such experiences for no obvious reason and with no intentional efforts to do so. If attaining this pure state of cosmic awareness actually required the mastery of complex constructs or years of effort and sacrifice, such spontaneous transformational peak experiences and unexpected transcendental consciousness events simply would not occur. The fact that they do occur spontaneously and with considerable regularity suggests that this experience actually is rather natural and not all that difficult to create. Such events imply, again, that every normal human brain may have the potential to experience this mode of consciousness under the right circumstances.

Whether all of us have an underlying ability to experience the world this way or not, all of us have good reason to want to do so. Even a brief or faint taste of such mystical or transcendental experiences seems to change people in dramatically positive ways. One momentary immersion can change a person's psychological and emotional condition forever, perhaps even altering basic hormonal, neurological, and biochemical states. In the same way that a brief but intense trauma can produce permanent physiological, psychological, and emotional changes characteristic of a post-traumatic reaction, it is possible that a brief but intense mystical experience can produce long-term emotional, psychological and physiological changes characteristic of improved mental health and happiness.

Whereas cognitive therapy attempts to chip away at negative and self-defeating attitudes one at a time, mystical experiences involve the creation of an entirely new view of the world all at once. This new view is exuberantly positive and joyfully optimistic. As a result of this sudden alteration in perspective, many different aspects of life become easier, everyday hassles become less important, anger diminishes, tension releases, pain disappears, and the person begins to feel "weller than well". Amusement and aesthetic pleasure replace irritation and dissatisfaction. Wisdom and compassion replace confusion and fear. Spontaneous thought, imaginative solutions, and creative action replace stress and the force of habit. Joy and playful amusement replace sadness and worry. Love and compassion replace selfishness and social isolation. Absorbed fascination and peaceful delight replace distracting concerns. Little wonder, then, that we tend to be drawn toward such states of mind. The potential benefits are obvious.

As a psychotherapist I am drawn toward such experiences for professional as well as personal reasons. For one thing, the goal of merely getting people back on their feet, restoring them to their previous level of functioning, or helping them become "good enough" to get by, has never been good enough for me. Instead, I am interested in helping people maximize performance, use previously unused potentials, access their inner resources, and begin feeling that life is both wonderful and full of wonder. That is what I want for myself, and that also is what I want for my clients. In this regard, exposure to a mystical experience is often like the decorative icing on a therapeutic cake, a finishing touch that gives special meaning to the entire process.

On the other hand, such experiences can be the cake itself. Moments of mystical consciousness or spiritual awareness can provide core therapeutic breakthroughs or even serve as the total therapeutic experience. The cognitive, emotional, and physiological consequences of such events are so intensely transformational that they can, at times, permanently replace major depression, anxiety, and even chronic pain, with pleasure and comfort. In addition, there are numerous informal reports that such experiences have resolved significant behavior problems such as drug and alcohol addictions, smoking, and compulsive gambling. I strongly suspect, based on my own personal observations and experiences, that these and other effects are not the result of any conscious therapeutic "insights", but instead reflect a cascade of significant and permanent changes in physiological function, neurological structure, or perhaps even in the responses of individual cells and the levels of various neurotransmitters.

Although any psychophysiological sources of the therapeutic benefits produced by these critical moments are unknown and quite debatable, the benefits themselves seem to be thoroughly recorded and well-established. After such experiences the pains and problems of everyday life just do not seem as important, upsetting, or engaging. Accordingly, this book enthusiastically encourages professional therapists and counselors to incorporate such "mystical" experiences into their practices.

At the same time, however, I see no reason why people ought to be required to consult a highly paid professional if they want to pursue such experiences. Human beings have been experiencing the benefits of peak or mystical events on their own for centuries with few, if any, ill effects and a great many beneficial ones. They also have been experiencing the focused attention typical of meditative and hypnotic "trances" for thousands of years. Thus, I maintain that it is possible for almost everyone to learn how to use hypnotic procedures, such as those demonstrated in this book, to liberate the natural self-healing abilities and problem-solving potentials of themselves and others. There are no special magical incantations or dangerous rituals and phrases involved in these procedures. Anyone who has ever captivated a child's imagination with a fairy tale or entertained a group of friends with a story about a humorous incident has already used the same processes used in the hypnosis scripts presented in this book. If you know where you want to take yourself or someone else, all you need to be able to do is to describe that place as fully, completely, and comfortably as possible. The mind will follow a captivating description of a balloon ride upwards toward the tops of white billowing clouds just as quickly and easily as it will sink gently down like a pebble into the quiet warm depths of a calm clear pool.

Each hypnosis script presented in this book demonstrates a complete trance session. Thus, each script begins with a trance induction, progresses through a semi-coherent set of direct and indirect (or metaphorical) suggestions, and ends with a trance termination process, though it is often difficult to tell exactly where one stage begins and the other ends. All of these sessions are examples of procedures I have used previously to induce hypnotic trances and to prompt episodes of cosmic consciousness in myself and/or others. Although each session is designed to help the mind move toward a cosmic or peak experience, each also takes a different route toward that goal. It is hoped that providing this smörgåsbord of possibilities will demonstrate that there is no absolutely right path to take toward the desired end state, no magical incantations or rituals that must be followed precisely by everyone. It is also hoped that providing this smörgåsbord of possibilities also will insure that everyone can find a path that feels comfortable and appropriate.

In this regard, it must be emphasized that these scripts are not designed to replace or override personal preferences, subjective reactions, and individual differences. The scripts and suggestions offered here are only general guidelines or exemplars based on my own research, my reading in the field, personal experiences, observations while working with others, and conversations with fellow professionals. Every individual responds differently to such procedures and, ideally, these different patterns of response will be acknowledged and used for direction or guidance. The psychological and emotional benefits of cosmic consciousness are incredibly enticing, but any approach toward that goal state should be designed to be as comfortable as possible. If anything begins to feel awkward or unpleasant, it is appropriate to stop, back up, and try a different path.

I do not know of anyone who has managed to become continuously immersed in transpersonal bliss, nor am I convinced that this would be a good idea even if we could do it. As Zen masters point out to their students, before enlightenment one must chop wood, carry water, and wash dishes; after enlightenment one must chop wood, carry water, and wash dishes. The chores and activities of ordinary life must continue on.

Nor is the journey toward cosmic awareness ever done. Just as cloth gradually becomes a deeper and deeper shade of red with each immersion in a bath of natural dyes, each immersion in an altered state intensifies the experience, takes us a step closer – but we never really arrive. Those who believe that they have arrived are probably just momentarily deluded. They will get over it eventually.

On the other hand, merely starting down the path toward that ephemeral mystical state is a pleasure and gaining even fleeting glimpses of it can leave one glowing for days. I hope and trust that my efforts will help you move yourself and others a few more steps forward along that path into the embrace of everlasting peace and harmony. I also hope that you will share with me any insights you might be able to contribute to this quest. Comments, observations, personal vignettes, case examples, criticisms, suggestions, etc. are all welcome and may be sent to me at:

Havens.Ronald@uis.edu
or
Ronald A. Havens, PhD
Department of Psychology
University Hall – Room 3144
One University Plaza, MS UHB 3144
University of Illinois at Springfield
Springfield, IL 62703-5407

Introductory Disclaimers
and Qualifiers

While writing this book I participated in various professional conferences or workshops where I agreed to present brief summaries of my efforts in creating mystical experiences. Interest in the topic was high, attendance typically was standing room only, and the enthusiasm of the audience was apparent. Paradoxically, it was just this interest and enthusiasm that invariably led someone in the audience to offer a pronouncement about what is "really happening" during these experiences, what we "should" call them, or what types of people "should" be encouraged or even "allowed" to have them. Although these comments seemed to stem from deeply held religious beliefs, strong personal sensitivities, and various personal experiences, I did not agree with them at that time and I do not agree with them now. Nonetheless, they occurred with sufficient regularity that it would be inappropriate or foolish to ignore them entirely.

Accordingly, the following statements present some of the fundamental assumptions of this book that others might wish to challenge or question, acknowledge a few of the flaws and limitations of my efforts that others might otherwise feel compelled to point out, and present my obviously biased justifications and rationalizations for handling various issues the way I have. I do not anticipate that these preemptory comments will change minds or prevent criticism. I just want to begin this book by getting as many of these potential distractions out in the open and out of the way as possible.

Point I. This book is an open invitation to join me in my ongoing explorations of hypnotic pathways into an alternate experiential world. I maintain that this alternate world of inner peace and happiness is created by even a faint or momentary immersion in the infinite wisdom and unknown potentials that lie just beneath the surface of everyone's conscious awareness. It is a world far removed from the cares and concerns of contemporary life, a world where every thought is embedded in bliss, every perception is charmed by a sense of beautiful magic, and every sensation is a connection to everything everywhere. It is a world that soothes the soul, brings contentment, and heals wounded spirits.

I make no apologies for the enthusiastic extravagance of these descriptions of the desired outcome of the procedures presented in this book. Even a relatively unsuccessful effort to experience a state of mystical consciousness can be pleasantly relaxing and therapeutically beneficial. Accordingly, a high level of enthusiasm is more than warranted from my point of view.

At the same time, however, I also want to make absolutely sure that my enthusiastic commitment to the topic is not mistaken for a naïve acceptance of supernatural spiritualism. I want to make it clear that the approach presented in this book does not involve or even acknowledge, much less depend upon, concepts such as ESP, psychokinesis, channeling, psychic powers, clairvoyance, reincarnation, past life regressions, ghosts, gods, poltergeists, fairies, angels, elves, alien abductions, spirit guides, magnets, crystals, or copper bracelets. I am firmly convinced that the alterations of consciousness dealt with throughout this book merely involve a different (although in some ways, perhaps, a more open or valid) way of perceiving the world, not a way of tapping into some mythical external Universal Mind, and are most certainly not a source of superhuman powers or supernatural energies.

My foundation position is that the experiences described in this book are generated by and occur totally within the brain. I do not believe that we are tapping into some external source of light, energy, or wisdom, nor do I believe that we are opening a connection to one god or another or communicating with the spirit of some ancient guru or ancestor – although that obviously is how many people have interpreted such experiences in the past. No matter how it "feels" or what it reminds us of, I have no reason to believe that what we are experiencing during a mystical episode (or during any type of so-called "psychic" or "supernatural" event for that matter) is anything other than what the brain is inherently capable of generating and experiencing on its own. In my opinion, to suggest otherwise is to move into a delusional realm that has the potential to be counterproductive at best and, at worst, encourages us to overlook and even deny the incredible power, intelligence, and wisdom lying dormant within the unconscious of us all.

On the other hand, I recognize that my opinion is not going to change the mind of those who believe in the supernatural origins of such experiences any more than their opinion is going to change mine. My puny skepticism is not going to seem very persuasive to someone who believes that "God" came to them during a profound mystical episode. My belief that what they experienced was an awareness of the untapped "godliness" within us all just does not have the same pizzazz or appeal as an encounter with the Creator. I understand that and respectfully suggest a truce, therefore, a peaceful coexistence. Instead of wasting time and energy debating the underlying nature or source of such experiences, let us focus, instead, on how to help everyone access these experiences and benefit from the enormous potentials they seem to offer.

Point II. I purposefully chose to use a variety of terms throughout this text for the epiphany experiences and altered states I am pursuing here. Thus, although I do tend to use the terms cosmic consciousness, mystical experience, and enlightenment most of the time, at any given point I might instead choose to use a term such as peak experience, spiritual awareness, mystical insights, pure consciousness, or transcendental awareness. I could equally well refer to this state as rapture, nirvana, revelation, transpersonal consciousness, illumination, rebirth, satori, nirvana, moksha, atma-bodha, transcendent consciousness, ishwara, ecstasy, epiphany, spiritual transformation, spiritual unity, spiritual insight, ecstatic visions, visionary experiences, contact with God, mystical awareness, angelic journeys, or immersion-in-the-absolute. I use these terms interchangeably because I believe that all of them refer to similar, if not identical, alterations of experience and awareness. Even near-death experiences are similar in many ways to intense cosmic consciousness episodes.

My somewhat arbitrary or seemingly capricious use of these various terms as if they are interchangeable may annoy or even offend some people. They would argue, and perhaps rightfully so, that these descriptors are not entirely interchangeable because each was created to describe a different experience produced by a different religious practice in a different culture. On the other hand,

I am dumping all of these terms into the same pot throughout this text because I am convinced that the experiences they each describe are much more similar than different. In fact, I maintain that in spite of superficial differences, they are all essentially identical. This is another foundation construct of this book. I realize that this may place me in the realm of the "perennial philosophers" such as Gottfried Leibniz, Aldous Huxley, William James, Abraham Maslow, and Huston Smith, but this seems like pretty good company to me and, thus, I intend to embrace it fully.

The mystical experiences of one individual are necessarily somewhat different from those of another. Even the various mystical experiences of any one person will differ from one another to some extent. Some peak experiences involve overwhelmingly intense insights into universal truths while others may involve little more than a profound appreciation for the beauty and perfection of a flower or a particular sculpture. It is not surprising, therefore, that different people in different cultures at different times have devised a variety of different terms in an effort to capture or convey a particular aspect of their own particular "mystical" or "cosmic" experiences.

On the other hand, the similarities between the experiences referred to by these various terms far outweigh the differences. All of these experiences seem to emanate from essentially the same types of brain activity, involve essentially the same sensory, emotional, and intellectual effects, and produce essentially the same psychological and emotional outcomes. Each term refers to an experience of an explosively intense, usually brief, but seemingly endless immersion in an inexpressible awareness of the interconnected unity and beautiful perfection of some particular thing, whether that thing is a rose, a thought, or a universe. Accordingly, I intend to treat these various terms as functional equivalents. To do otherwise with a group of terms that all refer to an overarching sense of integrative oneness simply seems inappropriate and even absurd to me. In fact, I find it amusingly paradoxical that anyone could, with a straight face, insist upon differentiating between various types of experiences of "integrative oneness".

Unfortunately, my amusement in this regard must be tempered and diminished somewhat by the realization that historically such arguments have led to numerous armed conflicts and much suffering or death. Fundamentalist arguments over whose mystical unification experiences are the best or most righteous can and have become incredibly violent. If anything, however, such conflicts only enhance my determination to treat all such experiences as equal and to use all relevant terms interchangeably.

Point III. I have spent most of my professional career focused on the topic of hypnosis. As a result, the scripts I present here have "hypnotic" qualities. This simply means that they contain various verbal stratagems that were originally designed, primarily by Milton H. Erickson, MD, to capture and redirect attention in ways that enable people to become imaginatively involved with particular thoughts, images, sensations, or other internal events.

The approach used in the scripts presented in this book is "hypnotic" in the same sense that a good story or an effective guided imagery approach is "hypnotic" or captivating. It does not involve magic incantations or secret words having special powers. It does not create a mindless, robotic, automatically obedient state. It will not and cannot force anybody to experience anything. The approach presented here is designed simply to help people learn how to relax, to focus their attention, to become more accepting of unusual experiences, and to take unusual advantage of the often hidden abilities of their own "unconscious" potentials and creative imaginations.

Instead of calling them "hypnotic scripts", you may prefer to call them "guided imagery scripts", "autogenic suggestion scripts", "directed imagination scripts", or even "captivatingly poetic metaphors, similes, and anecdotes". As noted above, I do not take such verbal differentiations too seriously. In fact, I am not entirely sure that there are any real differences between a good guided-imagery session, a good story, and a good hypnotherapy session, so it certainly makes no difference to me what you call the approach used here.

It also makes little difference to me who uses the approach presented here. Although professional hypnotherapists and psychotherapists who have used guided imagery or hypnosis extensively may be more comfortable using this approach to help others than will therapists who have little experience in these areas, virtually anyone can use the approach presented here to stimulate the imagination of others. As noted in the Preface, if you have ever captured someone's attention with a good story, even if it was a bedtime fairytale, then you already have used at least some of the "hypnotic" techniques demonstrated in my scripts.

Along the same lines, anyone who has ever "gotten lost" for a time in a fantasy daydream or a reverie while driving or staring out a window can experience the kinds of events described in the scripts presented here, and that probably means virtually everyone can do it. There is nothing inherently difficult or dangerous about these procedures, they are just a natural, albeit unusual, extension of perfectly ordinary human abilities and capacities. The goal may be mystical, but the process of getting there is surprisingly ordinary, even somewhat mundane.

Point IV. I would like to take this opportunity to point out that this book is a practical guide based on my professional opinions and experiences, not an academic review, a scientific investigation, or a scholarly treatise. Rather being a detached and coldly objective analysis of the topic, it is an admittedly subjective and shamelessly autobiographical discussion of my personal explorations and conclusions regarding hypnosis, consciousness, and mystical experiences. It does not offer a detailed historical account of mystical events, a careful cataloging of the various references to light and spiritual energy in religious writings or other documents, nor does it present a thorough discussion of the current empirical research and theory regarding either altered states of consciousness or hypnosis. This text also does not acknowledge the many others in the field who have previously linked imagined immersions in light or fields of energy to beneficial psychophysiological changes and it does not provide a thorough review of relevant recent neurophysiological studies.

Such omissions do not a reflect a lack of relevant information. There are volumes of information available on each of these topics. There is so much, in fact, that even a cursory coverage of this material would be far beyond the scope and intention of this brief text. Besides, my goal here is not to use the available literature to justify and persuade. My goal is simply to present a set of ideas and techniques that I have found to be personally and profession-ally useful in the hope that they will prove to be useful for others as well.

Point V. A few authors have compared mystical or spiritual expe-riences to psychotic episodes and neurological anomalies, such as temporal lobe seizures. Although it may well be the case that some so-called mystical or peak experiences have been the result of psy-chotic or seizure-induced hallucinations, there is no reason to sus-pect that it might work the other way around, that induced or spontaneous mystical experiences in an otherwise normal individ-ual could precipitate either a psychotic breakdown or a seizure. I am quite sure that the experiences presented here are not potent enough to cause anyone to become psychotic or to have a seizure.

On the other hand, individuals with psychotic or delusional ten-dencies might be inclined to interpret any mystical experiences in rather bizarre ways. This may be the reason that some sects have cautioned against immersion in a mystical experience before mas-tering a specific set of meditative practices, reading a specific col-lection of texts, or experiencing a specific type of training. Their claim is that people have to be thoroughly prepared or completely ready to enter a mystical experience or else they will lose their way, wander from the path of righteousness, or perhaps become seduced by the "dark side".

It is conceivable that someone with delusional or a grandiose ten-dencies might begin to believe that their mystical experience is an indication of special powers, like ESP, or a sign of a special con-nection to god, just as they are predisposed to misinterpret any experience. As a result, even though I have never encountered such a negative consequence and even though the approaches pre-sented here are designed to avoid or negate such misinterpreta-tions, I strongly recommend against their use with or by such individuals.

Point VI. The odds are that your first experience with this approach will not be the kind of "mind-blowing" experience you were hoping for or expecting. Hypnotic techniques are not the same as psychedelic drugs. They do not *force* people to experience things; they merely *invite* people to experience things. Some people are ready and able to accept that invitation, but others are not. Responses are difficult to predict.

As a result, the experiences generated by the hypnotic approaches described in this book can range from relatively mild and seemingly temporary states of relaxation to intense bursts of overwhelming sensation, or even to profound alterations in thought or understanding. In some cases it may seem as if nothing at all has occurred, and yet the person's life over the next several days or weeks may be filled with unusual insights and perceptions. In other instances, there may be a deeply moving experience but no obvious aftereffects whatsoever. Even when exactly the same suggestions are used with the same person on different days, the outcome probably will be different. There are no guarantees or standardized outcomes when it comes to hypnotically directed alterations in subjective experiences. That is why I prefer to sit back, relax, enjoy whatever happens and be grateful for it, and why I invite you to do the same.

Point VII. Finally, I must note that these scripts were designed for use with adults and, thus, are not appropriate for use with children. Tempting though it may be to offer some of the experiences presented in this book to them, I strongly recommend against it and urge you to avoid doing so.

Section I

Background & Conceptual Orientation

Tempting though it may be to skip the concepts and information presented in the following chapters and to proceed directly to the scripts presented in Section II, I urge you to resist this temptation. A thorough understanding and successful utilization of the hypnotic scripts presented in Section II is more likely if you first allow me to explain what they are designed to accomplish and why.

Chapter 1

Lighting the Way

That's one small step for a man,
one giant leap for mankind.
—Neil Armstrong, 1969

Therapeutic change typically involves a step-by-step accumulation of small, almost imperceptible differences over time. Change tends to be difficult, minimalistic, and slow. But people can, at times, take a giant leap forward. They can develop a profound insight or create a deeper understanding. They can transcend their past and become a "new" person. They can shed old worries and enter a state of perpetual peace. They can jump ahead of themselves into a completely new future and invent solutions to problems they did not even know existed. They can do all of this and more in one brief but monumental moment of ecstatic bliss and passionate wonder.

Peak or cosmic experiences involve intensely overwhelming alterations in perception, thought, and emotion. They flood the body with a sudden rush of light, energy, or sound. They plunge the mind into a state of awe and wonder. They transform the mundane into a miracle. They then disappear as suddenly as they appeared, leaving behind a fertile opportunity for new growth and significant change. Just one of these experiences can lead a person off in a completely new direction. A whole series of them can lead someone off into a completely new identity and a completely new reality. The changes precipitated by such events can be so extensive that Miller and C'de Baca (2001) coined the term "quantum change" to convey their impact.

I wrote this book because I believe that enabling people to have such intensely therapeutic peak experiences is a legitimate goal of psychotherapy. In fact, I maintain that such transformational epiphany experiences should be made available to everyone on a regular basis. Thus, in this book, I describe how to use various hypnotic techniques (including self-hypnotic techniques) to move your own mind or the mind of someone else toward these mystical or cosmic consciousness states.

Because cosmic or mystical experiences can have such profound therapeutic effects, it is a bit surprising that procedures to stimulate them are not already an inherent part of every psychotherapist's practice. What makes this even more surprising is the fact that this is not a new or original idea at all.

My Pursuit of Cosmic Consciousness

It has now been over 30 years since I began investigating the possibility of using trance to stimulate the higher state of mind that various authors have referred to as "ecstasy", "spirituality", "transcendental consciousness", "cosmic consciousness", "mystical enlightenment", or "peak experiences". My interest in this topic began in the 1970s when I attended a presentation on spirituality and hypnosis by Bertha Rodger, MD, during an American Society of Clinical Hypnosis conference. I had never met or even heard of Dr Rodger and had no idea who she was, but the moment this radiant, white-haired, grandmotherly apparition with a beatific smile and a playful twinkle in her eyes entered the room, I knew she was our session leader.

At the time I was in the process of finishing my dissertation on the use of modeling to alter hypnotizability and was in the middle of my internship as a doctoral student in clinical psychology. I thought I knew all there was to know about hypnosis and about therapeutic moments, but I was about to find out that I was wrong. Dr Rodger gave a brief lecture on her use of hypnosis for anesthesia and spiritual healing in a hospital setting and then led the audience through the type of induction and suggestion processes she was then using with her patients.

I was not particularly responsive to hypnotic suggestions back then, in spite of my interest in the field, and as a result my reactions to her suggestions probably were pretty mild compared to the responses of the other audience members around me.

4

Nonetheless, when she described a light in the distance growing brighter and brighter, coming closer and closer, I could imagine seeing it reasonably clearly. And when she added a soft chorus of voices growing louder and louder, I could imagine hearing that as well. As that intense light and those harmonious sounds began to surround me, to engulf my awareness, I suddenly felt a rush of energy, a tingling surge of sensation and emotion throughout my entire body. Rather than riding that wave of energy, however, I quickly pulled myself out of it. It was too intense, too disorienting for me; it was more of a high than I was able to tolerate, it was a more rapid ascent into a field of pure consciousness than I could stand at that time. Nonetheless, this relatively brief but powerful episode was enticing enough to have long-term, life-changing consequences.

After that session I was intrigued. Even though the experience was essentially intolerable, it also was too intense to ignore. Over the next few weeks and months I began to feel somewhat dissatisfied. Like a potential addict who had just received a taste of bliss, I wanted more of that experience and I also wanted to find out how to help others experience it as well.

I already believed that therapy can happen in an instant. I had read about, experienced, and even created one or two "therapeutic moments" (those sudden flashes of insight or changes in perspective that are prompted by what often is an otherwise innocuous comment, action, or situation). I also was familiar with Abraham Maslow's work on the therapeutic value of peak experiences, and had, quite unintentionally, entered such states several times myself.

But what I experienced with Dr Rodger that day was a change in consciousness unlike anything I had ever experienced before. In hindsight it felt like I was dissolving into the underlying energy of the universe and becoming unrestrained emotionally, perceptually, and intellectually. Although this impression was derived from just a brief step across the threshold, from a momentary and somewhat terrifying plunge into that altered state of mind, I began to wonder if such experiences could be therapeutically useful. I also began to wonder if I could use hypnosis to precipitate similar alterations in consciousness.

5

One might think that the logical thing for me to do at that point would be to do exactly what Dr Rodger did, use hypnosis to immerse people, myself included, in an intense white light. But like any well-indoctrinated, left-brained social science graduate student, I first needed to *understand* what I was doing, to have a rationale or a theory for it. Consequently, rather than blindly following Dr Rodger's lead, which would have been the logical and most productive thing to do, I did what I was trained to do instead. I began reading and thinking.

I read about mysticism, spirituality, Buddhism, Zen, and Taoism. I read books by Alan Watts, D. T. Suzuki, Thomas Merton. I read William James' book, *The Varieties of Religious Experience* (1902/1929) and *The Cloud of Unknowing*, as translated by Ira Progoff (1957). Eventually I discovered *Cosmic Consciousness* by Richard Bucke (1900/1974), and John White's remarkable collection of essays on the topic (*The Highest State of Consciousness*, 1972). Finally, Charles Tart's *Altered States of Consciousness* (1969) contained a chapter by Arthur Deikman entitled, "Deautomatization and the Mystic Experience", which, along with the dual mind view proposed by Robert Ornstein in *The Psychology of Consciousness* (1972), essentially defined and directed my thinking about the nature and source of transcendental experiences for the next 30 years.

Eventually, based upon my reading in the field, I forgot all about the light and became convinced, instead, that cosmic or mystical consciousness experiences are created by a momentary loss of a sense of self, a dissolving of the Ego, an evaporation of the restrictions ordinarily imposed by the conscious mind's language-based construction of reality. I want to make it clear that this was not my idea. It was a conclusion based on the thinking of many others at the time. Various renowned "thinkers" had decided that getting rid of the thinking Self was the key to transcendence, and I thought that this idea made a lot of sense. After all, this conceptualization seemed to be consistent with the available research at that time on brain wave patterns (alpha waves) during meditative states and with the dominant theories of consciousness at the time as well. Accordingly, the elimination of thought, the evaporation of the Self, became my goal.

The first time I tried suggesting the disappearance of the Self to a hypnotic subject, however, the end result was anything but a mystical episode. Instead, the young woman in question reacted with a burst of anxiety and an immediate reorientation to wakeful awareness. Oddly enough, it had not occurred to me that experiencing the Self suddenly "disappearing", even imaginatively, might not appeal to everyone. It apparently seemed a bit too much like "dying" for her taste.

This incident suggested the need for a more gentle approach. Accordingly, I decided to conduct a survey to determine what hypnotically induced experiences people are able to tolerate most easily. What I found probably will seem intuitively obvious to you. What I found is that people do not like the idea of losing abilities, perceptual capacities, or personal orientation in time and space but they do like the idea of having their perceptual acuities increased.

I subsequently used this data to construct a series of trance sessions that led participants very gradually from relatively mundane, easily accepted enhancements and alterations of their inner experiences toward potentially more threatening losses of perception, orientation, cognition, and self identity. I then solicited volunteers and led them through the graduated series of sessions I had developed. The end result was that a majority of participants actually did report mystical types of experiences following the suggested loss of a sense of self and these experiences were then followed two weeks later by descriptions of relatively minor but positive changes in emotion, attitude and behavior.

I reported these promising, and admittedly highly preliminary, results during the Annual Convention of the American Society of Clinical Hypnosis, held in St Louis, Missouri, in 1978, and eventually published an article about them in the *Journal of Humanistic Psychology* (Havens, 1982). The response to these two reports was, quite literally, overwhelming.

I received hundreds of requests for reprints of my presentation and my article from people all over the world and from all walks of life. I was inundated by requests for audiotapes of the trance sessions I had used and most requests noted that price was not a concern. Several people even traveled across the country to my private practice office in order to experience cosmic consciousness for themselves.

I was thoroughly unprepared for such enthusiasm and uncomfortable with the notion that a neophyte like myself could suddenly become a sought after expert regarding such an esoteric and almost sacred phenomenon. The universality and intensity of the thirst for cosmic consciousness surprised me. I had only just begun exploring the experience myself and was not at all confident that what I had to offer at that point was worth all that fuss. After all, my research, although published, was just a pilot study and not a well-controlled assessment of the effectiveness of these procedures overall.

Furthermore, I was well aware that most approaches to hypnosis are relatively ineffective. Only a small percentage of the general population responds well to a traditional hypnotic induction and suggestion process. Although I had begun to explore a more promising hypnotic approach, one developed by Milton H. Erickson and his followers, I was not yet completely comfortable with it. I was not convinced that I even knew how to enable everyone to experience a trance, much less use that trance state to then eliminate a sense of the Self.

At the same time I was, paradoxically, slightly terrified that my approach would actually work. The intensity of interest others expressed in the experience combined with the intensity of the experience itself seemed potentially volatile and dangerous to me. It all just seemed like too much too soon, and I eventually decided to suspend my work with cosmic consciousness and to concentrate instead on developing my understanding of hypnosis. In hindsight, I am rather glad I did. The intervening years were quite productive and very rewarding.

Over the next two decades I authored and co-authored several textbooks, book chapters, and journal articles on Ericksonian approaches to hypnosis and hypnotherapy, and also offered many professional training workshops and lectures on hypnosis and hypnotherapy as well. And whenever I thought about returning to my search for a way to create cosmic consciousness, I typically reminded myself that I still had a lot to learn about hypnosis before I could again move in that direction.

This pattern of defensive avoidance changed dramatically several years ago when I was confronted by a series of professional, personal, and family crises. Just as I began dealing with one, something else would happen. The cumulative effect of these jarring consecutive emotional traumas was quite overwhelming and debilitating. My autonomic nervous system went into overdrive and stayed there. I became distracted by perseverative thoughts about the unresolved crises going on in my life, lost my appetite, was unable to sleep, unable to concentrate, and unable to relax. I felt anxious and stressed. All of my efforts to relax, to meditate, to use self hypnosis, and to redirect my thoughts toward the positive things in life proved fruitless. My condition threatened my ability to effectively carry out my responsibilities as a professor and a psychotherapist. I needed to get back on track and I needed to do it quickly.

As I pondered what to do about my situation one evening, I suddenly found myself thinking about an ex-student of mine named Helen. At first I did not understand why Helen had come to mind so forcefully, but eventually my thoughts about her led me back to the light, quite literally.

Fifteen years earlier, several years after her graduation and long after I had stopped my work on mystical consciousness, Helen had called me and asked for my help with her intense pain. She had cancer, untreatable terminal cancer. During our first session I guided her into a trance and told her simply that her unconscious mind could now use the openness of her trance state to provide those things she needed. Within a few minutes she stiffed a bit, then smiled broadly and just sat there smiling for over 30 minutes.

Afterwards she explained that she had just been sitting there in a kind of blank waiting state when she began to feel surrounded by a warm light that became brighter and brighter and eventually became such an intensely brilliant light that the energy of it seemed to penetrate every cell in her body, at which point she could no longer tell where the light began and where she ended. She felt herself merge with the warm energy of that light, and then she "knew" that the light was everything around her, a vast unity of loving energy that is everything and everyone. She said that this "understanding" was followed by a feeling of overwhelming peace and by a realization that at that moment she was feeling no pain at all.

Helen was quite excited as she told me all of this afterwards and even cried a bit, apparently tears of happiness or joy. She said she was no longer afraid of death, and no longer afraid of her pain. I was later told that she continued to use trance on her own until her death a few months later.

Although I was fascinated and impressed by her experience at the time, I was not smart enough to put two and two together and to instantly realize that Dr Rodger was right ... that becoming immersed in an inner light is an effective pathway into a mystical state of mind. In fact, to be quite honest, Helen's experience did not remind me of my consciousness altering session with Dr Rodger at all. Instead, having previously set aside all thoughts about my work with cosmic consciousness, I merely bid Helen goodbye, said hello to my next client, and promptly forgot all about the somewhat miraculous event I had just witnessed.

As I began thinking about Helen's experience while in my "crisis mode", however, the similarity of her experience to my own experience with Dr Rodger suddenly became blatantly apparent. It had been right there in front of me the entire time! How could I have overlooked it? If you have ever torn your house apart looking for something, such as keys or glasses, and then found them lying out in the open on the kitchen counter right where you began searching, then you have some idea of how I felt. My ability to ignore the obvious stunned me. And to make matters worse, Helen was not the only example. As I thought more about it I began remembering examples of other clients who had entered the light and been saved in some way.

For instance, I was once asked by a colleague from the rehabilitation unit of a local hospital to see a WWII veteran who had been severely injured when a kamikaze pilot slammed into the ship he was on. He was thrown backwards into the bulkhead of the ship by the explosion. The impact broke his back in several places and damaged his liver and kidneys. Over the next few years he went through many operations and ended up with so much scar tissue wrapped around the nerves and tissues of his abdomen and back that he was now experiencing excruciating pain and virtually continuous muscle spasms.

I was supposed to use hypnosis to help this man manage his pain, but after talking to him for a short time I discovered that he was a lay minister and that his church taught that hypnosis is the work of the devil. Accordingly, I simply asked him to close his eyes, to stop fighting the pain, and to just listen to my voice while I explained a few things to him. I then told him that he had a conscious mind and an unconscious mind and that his unconscious mind could find a way for him to experience relief from his pain if he asked it to do so and gave it a chance to do so in the right way at the right time for him. I said this many times in many different ways and then I asked him if he understood and if he would agree to allow his unconscious to help him. He indicated he would, opened his eyes, noted that he already felt a little better, and left with a smile on his face.

Two weeks later he arrived at our next appointment quite excited and obviously pleased. He stated that he was feeling much less pain than before but that, more importantly, he had experienced no pain at all for an entire afternoon. He also said that this had not happened to him in the 40 years since he had been injured.

He had been sitting in his back yard with his eyes closed, relaxing the way he had relaxed while listening to me talk during our first session. He asked his unconscious for help and then all of a sudden, "It seemed like the clouds parted, and I felt a brilliant ray of sunlight come down into or through me, and it was as if the hand of God reached down and touched my back and took the pain away." It took away more than his physical pain. It also took away his severe chronic depression and left him feeling more joyful and full of life than he had in years. He returned to his ministry with renewed faith, vigor, and intensity.

Remembering these events one after another enabled me to actually begin to see the light, to finally realize that immersion in light is a rapid and perhaps natural route into mystical experiences.

Following this realization I re-read Bucke's description of his own mystical episode in his classic book from 1900, *Cosmic Consciousness*, and wondered once again how I could have overlooked something so blatantly obvious. Bucke wrote that while riding home after an evening reading poetry with some friends, he suddenly and without warning, "found himself wrapped around as it were by a flame colored cloud. For an instant he thought of fire, some sudden conflagration in the great city, the next he knew that the light was within himself. Directly afterwards came upon him a sense of exultation, of immense joyousness accompanied or immediately followed by an intellectual illumination quite impossible to describe" (Bucke, 1900, p. 8).

I also vaguely remembered and eventually looked up the description offered by Bill Wilson (one of the founders of AA) regarding his own healing enlightenment. As I thought, "Bill" stated that, "Suddenly the room lit up with a great white light. I was caught up in an ecstasy which there are no words to describe" (quoted in Delbanco & Delbanco, 1955). Again, there it was, the light that leads to ecstasy and personal transformation.

Finally, I reread several collections of essays that had played a crucial and deciding role in the development of my belief that the loss of the Self is the cause of mystical experiences. I found, for example, that although Deikman (in Ornstein, 1973) did argue that mystical experiences are produced by renunciation or annihilation of the Self, he also stated that, "Liberated energy experienced as light may be the core sensory experience of mysticism," p. 228). Similarly, after describing many techniques, including hypnosis, for the creation of "visionary experiences", Aldous Huxley stated that "The highest common factor, I think, in all these experiences is the factor of light" (presented in White, 1972, p. 47).

That evening I sat down, entered a mild self-hypnotic trance, began remembering my experience with Dr Rodger, and conjured up that same image of a bright light far off in the distance. As it got closer and closer I began to feel its energy, as I had before, until eventually that light surrounded me, entered me, and seemed to send spine tingling chills shooting through me like waves of soft electricity that expanded off into space in all directions. By that time, a chorus of sound that reminded me of the melding voices of a choir had blended with the energy surges I was already feeling.

The details of my subsequent experiences that night are not important here. The various descriptions of pure consciousness or spiritual enlightenment presented throughout this text provide an adequate account. The important thing is that I almost instantly began to feel much better and emerged from that experience with a renewed sense of calm contentment and a revived interest in developing ways to help others enter such states. The intensity of this disorienting consciousness alteration no longer worried or frightened me. Instead, it appealed to me as a potent indicator of a mind sweeping itself clean, transforming itself with a rush of clarity.

Unfortunately, at first, these experiences and insights simply switched my focus from "the loss of a sense of Self" to "immersions in light". Like a dog who has switched from chewing on and protecting one bone to chewing on another, I now began thinking that "light" was the one and only true answer. In spite of the fact that I had spent the past 30 years working within an Ericksonian framework which emphasizes individualization above all else, I immediately reverted to a "one-size-fits-all" approach. I began trying to immerse everyone in "light".

Not surprisingly, not everyone can see the light, not everyone likes the light, and not everyone needs the light. It did not take long for my clients to remind me that some people need or prefer sound, some prefer sensation, and some prefer a perceptual or conceptual immersion in perfection. People are not all alike. Light may predominate as an entry into a mystical state but it is not the only pathway.

A woman who had recently lost her daughter to suicide responded only to the imagined sound of a chorus of angels, not to light at all. She subsequently reported that as she became lost in the sound, she began to feel herself drifting along with it, and eventually thought she heard her daughter's voice among all the rest telling her that she was fine. This woman emerged from the trance feeling soothed and reassured by the experience.

A man in his 50s who was consumed by anger and wracked by arthritic pain in every joint eventually responded to a suggested rush of tingling sensations throughout his entire body, after which he was able to become the heat of a roaring fire, and eventually the sound and sensation of a cool and gently flowing mountain stream. Afterwards, his anger diminished and his pain subsided.

An accountant in his late 30s who had developed serious allergic responses to an enormous variety of natural and man-made substances during a period of intense stress five years previously did not react to anything I suggested during our session together, but apparently he did react to a post-hypnotic suggestion that his unconscious mind could provide him with a particularly pleasant experience sometime later that week. As he and his wife were driving to the grocery store, he was suddenly overwhelmed by the absolute beauty and perfection of the moment … the sunshine, the fall colors, the smell of dry leaves, the quiet contentment of being loved, of loving … all came together at once and connected him once again in a positive and comfortable way to the world around him. His allergic reactions diminished, became quite manageable, and eventually virtually disappeared.

These and other similar experiences helped me stop searching for the holy grail, for the one true approach, and enabled me to recognize what now seems blatantly obvious, that there probably are as many hypnotic routes into transpersonal or cosmic states of consciousness as there are people willing to experience such states. The key is that enlightenment occurs when there is an overwhelming immersion in a pleasurable sensation, perception or emotion. On the other hand, this typically only happens after the person has, for one reason or another, slipped into a trance state of mind, thus losing a sense of Self and becoming a blank, rather empty or objective observer of events. In other words, as I first thought, the loss of a sense of Self does indeed play a vitally important role. It sets the stage. But the cosmic experience itself occurs when that state is used to create something more, something more intense and overwhelming than would occur otherwise.

How to Use Hypnosis to Create Cosmic Consciousness

Thanks to the clients and friends of mine who were quite willing to tell me what worked for them and what did not, I am now convinced that every commonly reported component of cosmic or mystical experiences (including the inconceivably brilliant light, the rush of almost orgasmic tingling sensations, the penetrating harmonies, the powerful emotion of awe or wonder, and the inevitable immersion in the perfection and oneness of all things) is a potential point of entry into that state of mind. It now seems obvious to me that experiencing any one of these aspects of cosmic consciousness can trigger all of the other aspects of that state of mind in a cascade of events that eventually leads to the full experience.

Each separate quality or dimension of the enlightenment experience involves an overwhelmingly intense level of neural activity in some part of the brain, such as the visual centers, the auditory centers, or the sensory systems – which seems to be capable of stimulating that same level of intense activity throughout the rest of the brain and body. For whatever reason, this intensity produces a profound depth of awareness and understanding that transcends all previous conscious constructs. It is as if the mind is washed clean by a rush of unspeakably intense sensations and emotions. What remains is like an unspoiled wilderness, a purity of thought, perception, and reaction that is uncontaminated by ordinary conscious ways of thinking and open to a direct and uncensored awareness of events.

Thus the logic or rationale underlying the procedures presented here is really quite simple. To begin with, the loss of a sense of Self that is so frequently and universally associated with the occurrence of such mystical experiences actually is the development of a trance state. This "empty" and passively observant state of mind (hypnotic trance) is vitally important because it provides a reduced level of conscious interference and a correspondingly increased "suggestibility" or enhanced "imaginative involvement". These qualities, in turn, can then be used to alter perception, sensation, emotion, and thought in the direction of a mystical experience. Such modifications of sensation, perception and experience are, after all, the essence of hypnosis. Hypnotic trance is of value medically and therapeutically specifically because it can be used to alter perception and reaction. During a hypnotic trance suggestions can be used to help subjects experience almost anything, from the imagined pleasure of floating on a warm sun-lit cloud to the hallucinated comfort of stroking the soft fur of a purring cat.

Furthermore, these hypnotically produced changes in experience can create such vivid and complete imaginary simulations of the "real" thing that the end product may actually be experienced in the same way *as* the real thing. A hypnotically induced experience of being touched by something hot can create a startle reaction and even a change in the color of the skin. In some people it can actually create a blister. Similarly, a hypnotically induced experience of hearing a specific love song can create the same emotional and neurophysiological reactions as actually hearing that song. The parts of the brain involved in hearing actually fire at an increased rate when an imagined sound is "heard". This also applies to imagined sights, sensations, movements and emotions.

Hypnotically induced experiences seem real or compelling because they involve the activation or firing of the same neural circuitry as the real life event. When you "imagine" seeing something, the "seeing" part of your brain is activated. In fact, it engages in essentially the same pattern of activity that it would if it were actually seeing that thing. Similarly, when you imagine running, the parts of your brain involved in running are activated. There is even evidence to indicate that imagined practice of a physical skill, such as shooting a basketball, significantly improves mastery of that skill and that imagined exercise can actually strengthen a muscle to some small degree.

Accordingly, the central proposition of this book is that when we use hypnotic suggestions to create the kinds of thoughts and sensations that typically occur during a mystical state of enlightenment, we are creating essentially the same neurological, physiological, and experiential effects as the "real" thing. In other words, a clearly imagined mystical experience should be comparable to, perhaps even indistinguishable from, one that occurs for any other reason.

A calmly focused trance can be used to create an imaginary immersion in a brilliant white light, an angelic choir, a vibratory surge of sensation, or even a feeling of a cellular connection to the life force of every living creature on earth. The end result of such hypnotically induced phenomena is a close approximation physiologically and experientially of a "genuine" mystical event.

Stated simply:

1. **There is a consistent, holistic set of sensations, perceptions, and cognitions associated with "mystical", "peak", or "spiritual" experiences.**
2. **The open-minded imaginative involvement of hypnotic trance can be used to create specific sensations, perceptions, and cognitions.**
3. **Therefore, to create "mystical", "peak", or "spiritual" enlightenment experiences, use hypnotic suggestions to immerse the person in an imagined set of intense sensations, perceptions, and cognitions that are similar to those of any typical mystical, peak, or spiritual enlightenment experience.**

This simple three-part statement provides the rationale for this entire book. Unfortunately, just because the underlying rationale is simple, this does not mean that the concepts and procedures used to attain the desired outcome also are simple. Because people differ from one another in so many ways, there is no one "right" way to accomplish the goal desired. Accordingly, this book demonstrates a wide variety of somewhat generic approaches and invites the reader to peruse the options.

The Organization and Use of This Book

The remaining chapters in Section I provide a conceptual framework for understanding and using the scripts presented in Section II. Chapter 2 offers a detailed description of the goal state of cosmic consciousness and explains the potential short- and long-term benefits of this experience. Chapter 3 examines the unpleasant consequences of judgmental thinking and reviews the steps required to replace this type of thinking with a mystical state of mind. Chapter 4 looks at the relationship between the conscious and unconscious components of our mental life and relates these components to the experience of hypnotic trance. Chapter 5 presents a brief discussion of the nature of hypnotic trance and hypnotic suggestions and outlines the steps in a typical hypnotic procedure.

If you are already familiar with hypnotic or guided imagery techniques, the scripts presented in Section 2 can serve as guidelines that you may embellish or modify in whatever way is most suitable to your style and circumstances. Amplify whatever feels comfortable, eliminate anything that does not, and add whatever you like. In other words, use the scripts presented here as inspirational opportunities to create your own scripts for helping others shift into a transcendent state of mind.

Unfortunately, a sudden shift into a mystical state of consciousness can be a rather disconcerting alteration in awareness, even for someone who is an experienced hypnotic subject. At first people may feel a bit like the earth has suddenly fallen out from under them or as if they are tumbling in space. And then there is the almost inevitable surge of intense energy or emotion that usually accompanies these experiences. Entry into the state of mind and body associated with cosmic consciousness can be so disorienting and overwhelming that many people will simply pull out of it altogether the first time or two that they begin to enter into it, just as I did the first time I began to experience it with Dr Rodger.

To make matters even more problematic, a lot of people have difficulty just entering into a basic, internally focused hypnotic trance state, much less experiencing a more intense cosmic alteration of consciousness. Research consistently shows that 80% to 90% of the population is comparatively unresponsive to the traditional authoritarian or directive form of hypnosis seen in most movies and stage acts. This may be because people do not like being told what to do, cannot tolerate the idea of losing control as they relax into a trance, or do not like losing touch with the chattering of the conscious mind or Self, i.e. "dying". It also is possible, as some researchers have suggested, that the ability to respond to hypnotic suggestions, to enter into a state of focused attention and become imaginatively involved, is simply a very rare phenomenon.

Whatever the cause, the fact remains that not all approaches to hypnosis are effective with a majority of the population. Accordingly, all of the scripts presented in this text incorporate a variety of Neo-Ericksonian hypnotic approaches, such as allusions, double binds, puns, similes, metaphors and anecdotes to facilitate the trance induction and suggestion process. These and other verbal stratagems were specifically designed by Dr Milton H. Erickson (a psychiatrist who is widely acknowledged to be the most creative, effective, and insightful hypnotherapist of the 20th century) to capture attention, facilitate relaxation, and tap into unconscious abilities and resources that otherwise tend to go overlooked or unused. Because they are specifically designed to comfortably and automatically stimulate hypnotic changes in perception and imagination, these Neo-Ericksonian techniques are often able to facilitate hypnotic responses that might be difficult to obtain otherwise. As such, they are very useful tools for anyone interested in immersing themselves in or leading others towards significant, albeit imaginary, alterations in awareness and experience, including alterations of the type we are interested in here.

It must be noted, however, that this book does not contain a thorough description or explanation of the various direct and indirect Neo-Ericksonian hypnotic procedures used in the scripts presented here, nor does it offer detailed instructions for creating your own scripts. I have omitted such material because two of my previous books, each co-authored with Catherine Walters, (*Hypnotherapy Scripts: A Neo-Ericksonian Approach to Persuasive Healing* (1989/2002) and *Hypnotherapy For Health, Harmony and Peak Performance: Expanding the Goals of Psychotherapy* (1993)), already contain rather extensive explanations for and examples of these "Neo-Ericksonian" hypnotic techniques. In addition, another of my books, *The Wisdom of Milton H. Erickson* (1985/2003) provides a detailed examination of Erickson's original thoughts and ideas regarding the fundamental nature of human beings, of psychotherapy, and, of course, of hypnosis and hypnotherapy. Any or all of these books would serve as valuable resources for individuals who would like to pursue a more in-depth understanding and mastery of the Neo-Ericksonian hypnotic approach.

Another point worth mentioning here is that certain types of experiences seem to provide better or easier gateways into the mystical state for some people than for others. Some people respond more intensely or easily to visualizations, for example, whereas others are more comfortable experiencing vividly imagined sounds or sensations. Accordingly, the scripts presented in this text are organized by the particular sensory, cognitive, or perceptual pathways that they emphasize. Thus, the scripts presented in Chapter 6 focus on changes in visual experience whereas the scripts in Chapter 7 emphasize kinesthetic changes. Chapter 8 contains scripts that play with auditory components of the cosmic experience and Chapter 9 explores the appreciation of perfection. Each script in Chapter 10 directs people toward a feeling of love and Chapter 11 can be thought of as a capstone to the rest because it contains scripts designed to stimulate a direct connection to the entire universe.

Although each script concentrates on one particular component of the cosmic consciousness experience, each also eventually directs attention toward all of the other sensory and emotional components. Begin with an approach that focuses on whatever aspect of the experience is the most comfortable starting point for the participant and follow that path until it is possible to fill in the rest of the picture. Immersion in one or another of the common aspects of a mystical experience can be a delightful and rewarding experience, but when all of them come together at once, the end result is indeed cosmic.

Chapter 2

The Nature of Cosmic Consciousness

*The attainment of genuine perfection implies
a reversion to the original nature of man,
he will revert to a condition of childlike innocence,
he will revert to the unconditioned,
he will revert to his original simplicity.*
—Lao Tzu, *Tao Teh Ching*,
600 BCE

When a computer freezes up or stops working properly, it may be necessary to reboot it, to shut things down, wipe things clean, and start all over again. In a sense, that is the goal of the various "cosmic consciousness via hypnosis" procedures described in this book. The procedures presented here are almost literally designed to "reboot" the brain, to help it first become very quiet and then to send a tremendous surge of energy through it to start it up all over again.

Such an experience can allow people to start over without all of their old cares, concerns, explanations, and evaluative attitudes. It can allow them to momentarily forget the past and to return to their original way of being, to look at the world anew from an unconditioned, unbiased, and more liberated perspective. It can allow people to revert to their "original simplicity", to reverentially perceive the wonder of the moment and, thus, to stop wanting things to be other than what they can be.

There are many terms for this fundamental experience of timelessness, perfection, beauty, peace, truth, love, and oneness. As I noted in the "Introductory Disclaimers and Qualifiers" section at the beginning of this book, I tend to prefer "cosmic consciousness", "peak experiences", and "mystical states", but I also maintain that many other terms are equally appropriate because they all seem to refer to the same category or family of experience; they all consist of minor variations on the same theme.

Over the years various authors, including many previously mentioned (e.g. Bucke, 1901/1974; Deikman, 1969; Huxley, 1972; James, 1902/1929; Maslow, 1965, 1971, 1972; Miller & C'de Baca, 2001; Ornstein, 1972 and Smith & Tart, 1998), have compiled lists of what they believe to be the typical characteristics or elements of these various mystical, peak, or visionary experiences. Although a detailed review and discussion of each of these listings is beyond the scope or intent of this text, it also is essentially unnecessary because each author included essentially the same characteristics or ingredients. A reasonably comprehensive compilation of the common characteristics listed by all of these authors is presented below.

It is worth noting that the specifics of a mystical experience will vary in response to each individual's background, current situation, and beliefs. Thus, Buddhists might hear Buddhist chants, Christians might hear a choir, and Atheists might hear an orchestra, but all of them will hear a sound of overwhelming power and beauty. The particularities may be different, but underlying those differences are some basic components or common ingredients that seem to be universal.

What Are the Ingredients of Cosmic Consciousness?

The most commonly listed basic ingredients of cosmic consciousness, peak experiences, mystical states, etc. are the following:

1. Unusually intense, overwhelming, and almost unbearable sensations that are not directly attributable to actual external stimuli. These sensations may include:
   a. a blindingly intense or penetrating light of unknown origin or location and/or a brilliant aura or engagingly beautiful luminescent glow emerging from surrounding objects and people.

    b.   an angelic sound, usually of a beautiful and comforting voice or a harmonious chorus of voices singing or humming.

    c.   a tingling orgasmic rush or flush of feeling throughout the body, perhaps coupled with a feeling of warmth or a burst of goose bumps. A surge of restless energy in the muscles and internal organs also occurs at times.

    d.   a physical or kinesthetic disorientation, a feeling of floating, falling, drifting, or even flying and, on some occasions, a feeling of separating from the body entirely and filling the surrounding space.

2.   A sudden and powerful perception of or deep appreciation of the necessary interrelationships between beauty, order, perfection, unity and harmony, usually as applied to some event, object, person, thought, or situation. This aspect of the experience involves becoming aware that all of these qualities are equally present at that very moment and are fully interactive or completely dependent on each other. Something is perceived to be beautiful because all of its parts are perfectly unified in a harmonious manner and yet it is experienced as perfect because it is beautifully organized, and as orderly because it is harmonious. Each quality produces and depends on all of the others.

3.   A state of absolute awe, transcendent amazement, or stunned wonder at the complete "truth" or "rightness" of that particular event, object, person, or thought, as if it could not possibly ever be improved on and is somehow, as a result, quite sacred, profound, and awe-inspiring.

4.   A direct experiential awareness, understanding of, or insight into the complex, perfectly organized web or system of interconnectivity within which every thought, event, object, or person (including oneself) exists. The awareness of the unity of everything, which often includes an awareness of one's own place within that infinite web and within the entire universe.

5.   A blissfully non-judgmental, accepting, non-evaluative, all-inclusive point of view that produces a consequent feeling of boundaries dissolving, dichotomies evaporating, and

classifications collapsing in on themselves. Verbal and conceptual differentiations suddenly are seen to be arbitrary, meaningless, or even dangerous. Reality is accepted as it is, in all of
its glorious perfection, with all of its sacred idiosyncrasies and
amusing oddities.

6. A conviction that all of this represents a significant revelation,
a profound "aha", a deep new insight, a clarity of awareness,
or a revelatory glimpse into the true nature of some part of
reality, perhaps even all of it at once.

7. A flood of pleasurable emotions, ranging from a peaceful contentment to an exuberant joy and even a giddy happiness.
These emotions often merge with a sense that one is both completely loved and completely filled with love; love for and by
other people or love for and by the universe as a whole. At
times people are moved to tears and/or to laughter by these
feelings.

8. An absolute, complete, or total immersion in the experience.
Thoughts about everything else are completely displaced or
replaced for a time. All attention is focused on and absorbed
by the different aspects of this experience.

9. A loss of a clear sense of time, almost as if time has ceased to
exist altogether. The time spent in this state can seem like both
an eternity and a brief instant. Objectively speaking, the experience rarely lasts more than 30 minutes and typically lasts for
mere seconds or even fractions of a second. Subjectively, however, the experience is literally timeless and, thus, its length is
indeterminate and basically irrelevant. In a very similar and
related vein, there may be a loss of orientation in space as well.
The person simply stops being aware of where they are for a
time.

10. A passive or detached observation of experience with no sense
of control over or direct responsibility for most of what is happening. Once it begins, there is a kind of autonomous flow or
pull to this experience that just moves things along, the way
tipping one domino leads the rest to fall. The only thing left for
the person to do is to just sit back and watch things happen.

11. A momentary loss of any thoughts about or awareness of the "Self". It is as if the person has forgotten to stay oriented, not only for time and space, but also for Self. For the moment there is just a kind of generic or basic awareness, with no thought given to the "me" who is being aware and no thought that "I" should try to influence the course of events. Instead, there is simply an impersonal, identity-free state of mind or awareness intently observing whatever is happening at the moment.

Like the regional variations in recipes for salsa, the proportion and the intensity of these ingredients will vary from one experience to another. Some ingredients may not be a noticeable part of one person's peak experience at all, while those same ingredients may seem to stand out with a special potency on other occasions. Furthermore, some peak experiences will involve a focus on something that is a rather mundane part of daily life (e.g., a person, object, music, natural scene, etc.) while others will be directed toward more profound philosophical or religious concepts, perhaps even toward the nature of life or the universe itself. Finally, a person's imaginative involvement in the experience can be either highly intense or relatively detached.

Given these possible variations in intensity, focus, and content, it is not surprising that one mystical experience may lead to little more than a pleasant memory whereas another may ultimately generate dramatic life changes or even prompt the creation of a new religion. Not all mystical, peak, or cosmic experiences are created equal. Nonetheless, no matter what we call them or how different they are, they all have many of the same basic ingredients and, accordingly, they also all have many of the same basic short and long-term aftereffects.

What Are the Aftereffects of Cosmic Consciousness?

Immediate Aftereffects

In spite of potential variations from one instance to another, there are several fairly typical aftereffects of most cosmic consciousness experiences. The typical immediate aftereffects include:

1. People almost always recognize that this state of mind is quite different from ordinary wakeful awareness; it stands out as something "special" and as something they would like to repeat.
2. People typically feel grateful for their peak or mystical experiences. They appreciate the opportunity to participate in something so unusual, wondrous, and inherently valuable and they often are humbled by the experience, wondering aloud what they have done to deserve such a special privilege.
3. Along similar lines, mystical experiences often leave people with a newfound gratitude for the fact of being alive and, consequently, for being able to participate in such wondrous experiences. It may eventually seem that peak experiences are what make life worth living.
4. After a mystical experience, everyday hassles, annoyances, and problems no longer seem particularly important, serious, or worth becoming upset about. Worries and fears are replaced, at least for a time, by a feeling of amused, or even bemused, happiness.
5. People usually find it hard to describe what they have just experienced or to express what they have learned during that experience. It is as if language cannot adequately capture the sensations, perceptions, feelings, thoughts, or understandings involved. Either there are no words for "it" (whatever "it" is), or "it" occurs in a part of the brain that cannot or does not use words. In any case, all efforts to describe the various ingredients and effects of mystical experiences seem to be bound to fail in some respects. No matter how carefully worded a listing or description is (including this one) or how inclusive such efforts attempt to be, there are aspects of mystical experiences that people simply cannot translate into words.

Long-Term Aftereffects

If cosmic consciousness episodes had no additional consequences at all, they still would be a pleasant and valuable addition to anyone's life. But some cosmic consciousness experiences have long-term effects that go far beyond anything described so far. Cosmic or peak experiences can profoundly and permanently alter a person's basic ideas, attitudes, identity, and behavior. The specific types of long-term changes people have attributed to a mystical or cosmic episode include the following:

1. Dichotomous thinking (the creation of conceptual boundaries between extremes such as *good* and *evil*, *right* and *wrong*, *up* and *down*, *me* and *not me*) becomes difficult to take seriously. Such dichotomous differentiations suddenly seem relativistic, arbitrary, imaginary, and basically meaningless.

2. As the conceptual or imaginary boundary between themselves and others diminishes or vanishes, people develop a feeling of kinship or identity with others at a deep and elemental level. As a result, they become less judgmental, more empathetic, and more accepting. They also become less selfish and more generous or giving. Doing things for others becomes a source of genuine pleasure and personal satisfaction.

3. The experience of being connected, being one with others, not only elicits a loving, caring, and respectful attitude toward all people, but also toward life in all forms as well. People become aware of the similarities, rather than the differences, between people, animals, and life forms in general.

4. When this new non-judgmental, loving, accepting, and respectful attitude is directed toward the Self, people begin trusting themselves. They become less inhibited, less self-consciously restrained, less pretentious, more spontaneous, and more comfortable just being honest about what they think and who they are. They become able to accept and love themselves even though they possess a full awareness of their own limitations and foibles. People report that they begin feeling as if their thoughts and actions are guided or directed by an inner wisdom or an unseen but felt intelligence that is far greater and less confused than their ordinary conscious mind.

5. Life begins to seem beautiful and perfect, just the way it is, with all of its shortcomings and "problems". This occurs in spite of the fact that their perception of reality apparently also is more objective, less distorted, and less biased. People become more accepting of their own reality, happier with the way things actually are for them at that particular time, less driven by personal needs and desires. As a consequence, the simple events of everyday life seem to provide great pleasure and meaning.

6. Life also seems amusing to them, perhaps even silly or absurd. They enjoy playful antics, wordplay, and puns, but are put off by attempts at humor that involve hostility, violence, discrimination, or crudity.

7. Thoughts seem clearer, answers or creatively inventive solutions seem to spring to mind effortlessly, learning seems easier or more fun.

8. Anxieties diminish or disappear, replaced by a feeling of inner peace and calm, safe contentment.

9. Loneliness or any feelings of isolation fade into the past, even when a person is actually alone. Because mystical experiences leave people feeling connected to others, to all others, they also reduce the need to be around other people. Thus, paradoxically, even though such experiences lead people to become more comfortable around others, such experiences also tend to reduce the amount of time people actually spend around others. As they feel more connected, they also become more self-sufficient.

10. Everyday life becomes suffused with a feeling of liberation, a complete freedom to be and to do anything one wants. Along with this, however, comes a potent sense of responsibility for the consequences of all actions and for the ongoing creation of one's life circumstances.

11. Fear of death fades or vanishes. Different people provide different reasons to explain why they are no longer afraid to die. Some say that they now know they will never die because their essence, the spark of life and consciousness deep within them, is identical to that spark of life within each and every other person, or even every other life form, or, according to some, to every organized form of energy in the cosmos. As long as everyone or everything else continues to exist, so will they. Other people indicate that during their altered state of consciousness they talked to God, were touched by God, were reassured by God, or actually were taken to Heaven and, thus, already know what to expect. One way or another, fear of death diminishes and the person feels a tremendous sense of inner peace as a result.

12. Mystical experiences beget mystical experiences. The long-term changes in attitude, perception, and behavior created by mystical experiences make it more likely that mystical experiences will occur again in the future. Thus, for example,

experiences that lead to an enhanced appreciation of beauty, perfection, order, or unity, make it easier for the person to experience beauty, perfection, order, and unity in the future. Each mystical experience can be a life-changing experience in and of itself, but each mystical experience also sets the stage for or increases the probability of additional life-changing mystical experiences in the future. Thus, helping someone experience a mystical state is akin to planting a seed that will sprout and produce a tree that will then flower and produce additional seeds that will eventually spread to create an orchard or a forest.

Obviously, not all mystical events produce profound long-term or short-term effects of any type, much less all of the ones listed above. Just as these experiences vary in intensity and content, they also vary considerably in terms of the consequences they produce. The consequences will tend to vary proportionally to the intensity of the experience, but they also will tend to vary in response to the psychological and emotional readiness of the person having the experience. Cosmic consciousness experiences are a lot like seeds. How quickly they sprout and how prolifically they grow will depend on the climate and on the fertility of the soil where they fall.

Who Experiences Cosmic Consciousness?

The above lists of potential behavioral and psychological consequences of cosmic consciousness experiences bear a striking resemblance to Maslow's descriptions of the behavioral and psychological qualities of self-actualizing people (e.g., Maslow, 1965; Maslow, 1970; and Maslow, 1971). This is not a coincidence. Maslow discovered that people who are self-actualizing typically have had many peak or mystical experiences in the past and continue to have them regularly. He also noted that people who have had numerous peak experiences tend to become self-actualizers. Thus, the immediate and long-term effects of mystical or peak experiences on personality, beliefs, and emotions lead people toward self-actualization, and becoming more self-actualizing makes it more likely that that person will have future mystical experiences that will produce even more of the characteristics of self-actualization, etc.

29

This circular cause-effect relationship provides fertile ground for the creation of dramatic personal change over time. Even one brief or minor exposure to a cosmic or mystical state of mind can trigger minor changes in personality or outlook that will make future peak experiences somewhat more likely or more intense, and this increased frequency and intensity of peak experiences, in turn, may initiate a chain reaction of additional changes in personality and outlook that eventually will amount to a major personality transformation. On the other hand, it must be remembered that one significant or intense immersion in a mystical state of cosmic consciousness can precipitate a major personality transformation in a matter of moments. Some mystical experiences do "blow your mind".

No matter whether such personality alterations are a cumulative product of numerous minor peak experiences or a sudden transformation resulting from a mind-bending experience of cosmic proportions, the end product is quite similar. The end product is an individual who Maslow would classify as a self-actualizing person.

Although there are indications that most self-actualizing people have had and continue to have peak experiences on a fairly regular basis, there is no indication that you must be a mature, successful, self-actualizing person before you can have a mystical or peak experience. Indeed, examples abound of young, rather poorly adjusted individuals in dire straights who suddenly find themselves immersed in a cosmic consciousness episode. In fact, such experiences are often identified as the first step in a significant therapeutic rehabilitation process.

This is not meant to suggest that everyone is equally likely to experience a cosmic episode regardless of maturity or interest. Mystical states probably are potentially available to a majority of the population under the right circumstances, but there are many variables that make it easier for some people to experience such states than others. For example:

- At least average intelligence and a capacity for abstract reasoning are necessary.
- The higher a person's tolerance for ambiguity, the better.

- The higher the person's tolerance for unusual internal events (e.g., thoughts, images, sensations), the better.
- The greater the ability to enter a state of absorbed or focused attention, the better.
- An ability to relax physically and emotionally is helpful.
- A quiet, non-distracting environment is also helpful.
- Previous experience with peak or mystical experiences increases the probability of future peak or mystical experiences.
- Having personality characteristics typical of self-actualizers increases the probability of future peak or mystical experiences.

Obviously, individuals who already have had frequent spontaneous mystical experiences do not need a lot of additional help in this regard. Consequently, most of the scripts presented in this book were not devised with this relatively rare group of people in mind.

Similarly, the techniques contained in this book were not designed with people at the opposite end of the spectrum in mind, i.e., those who have never experienced a peak or mystical state, have no subjective sense of what it would be like to do so, and have little or no interest in doing so. The amount of explanation, reassurance, and assistance required in such cases is typically beyond the scope of the strategies presented here.

The hypnotic scripts and procedures presented in this book demonstrate an approach that can be used with that vast majority of people who fall somewhere between these two extremes, that is, with people who have a vague sense of and yearning for the inner peace and harmony of a mystical state of mind because they have had at least one brief glimpse of it. The approach presented here was designed to be used by and for people who know there are more comfortable or more effective ways of dealing with the world and want to find them, but are not sure of how to do so. It was created for individuals who may have had minor peak experiences in the past, but still have difficulty letting go and trusting their own unconscious abilities and potentials. It was developed for people who, like most of us, need an extra nudge or a push, some ongoing reassurance, and lots of direction in order to move into that higher, clearer, and more comfortable state of being, a state of being that is more fully alive and that is available to us all once we learn how to open the door into it.

Chapter 3

The Steps From Ordinary Awareness to Cosmic Consciousness

The mass of men lead lives of quiet desperation.
—Henry David Thoreau, *Walden*, 1854

It would be wonderful if everyone were immersed in a perpetual state of cosmic peace and enlightened tranquility. At present, however, it is quite obvious that this is not the case. Suffering, despair, and dissatisfaction appear to be much more widespread than cosmic consciousness. Even among religious fundamentalists, cosmic or mystical episodes still do not seem to be a common topic of conversation, much less a common goal in life, at least not in the United States.

Perhaps the most widely recognized and frequently discussed of all cosmic consciousness episodes anywhere is the one experienced in the sixth century BCE by an Indian Prince named Siddhartha. During a deep meditation session while sitting under a Bodhi tree, Siddhartha suddenly became immersed in an intense (reportedly a seven-day-long) state of mystical awareness that eventually transformed his understandings and changed him into Gautama Buddha, the founder of one of the largest religions and one of the most influential philosophies on Earth. Paradoxically, the main thing Siddhartha's cosmic experience provided was a profound comprehension, not just of beauty and pleasure, but of the nature and source of human misery and, more importantly perhaps, an appreciation for the way people could avoid or escape from the ongoing misery of their everyday lives.

In order to teach others the insights about life that he developed during his lengthy immersion in his cosmic experience, and thus free them from their suffering, Buddha eventually offered Four Truths to his followers. These Truths typically are translated in the following manner:

1. Life is pain.
2. Desire is the source of pain in life.
3. To eliminate pain, eliminate desire.
4. To eliminate desire, follow the Noble Eightfold Path (which involves the imposition of various controls over one's thoughts, actions, and feelings, as well as the regular practice of meditation).

Although typical, such a translation emphasizes a Westernized judgmental or puritanical attitude toward "desire" and this apparently is a misunderstanding or a distortion of Buddha's actual message. In 1958, Buddhist scholar A. J. Bahm offered what he felt to be a more accurate representation of Buddha's intended meaning:

> "Desire for what will not be attained ends in frustration; therefore to avoid frustration, avoid desiring what will not be attained." (Bahm, 1958/1969, p. 20).

According to Bahm, Buddha did not see desire itself as the source of our suffering nor did he suggest that people had to suppress all of their desires to become enlightened. Wanting things is not the source of suffering. Wanting things to be other than what they are and can be is the source of suffering and, thus, the way to avoid suffering is to avoid wanting things to be other than the way they are or can be.

This appears to be a logical and sensible prescription for relief from dismay, discouragement, disappointment and other forms of discomfort, but there are several major problems associated with it. Not only does it require people to accept the idea that their "wants" are responsible for their suffering, it also requires them to know how to change their wants and to accept or even admire the way things actually are and must be. None of these is an easy thing to do.

Buddha himself only reached his understanding of the relationship between desires and suffering after meditating regularly for years and finally becoming immersed within his own monumental session of cosmic consciousness. This same enlightenment experience also triggered his escape from desire and dissatisfaction into a state of pure bliss. It seems likely to me, therefore, that a mystical or cosmic episode probably still is one of the surest and quickest routes toward a release from irrational wants or desires and a joyful acceptance of the realities of everyday life. In fact, as I have mentioned before, mystical experiences seem to produce such an outcome almost automatically and that is exactly why I am interested in creating these states of mind.

My efforts in this regard have been heavily influenced not only by the story of Siddhartha's transformation into Buddhahood, but also by the teachings of Milton H. Erickson. In 1965 Dr Erickson gave a lecture in San Francisco during which he said:

> "Every patient who walks into your office is a patient that has some kind of problem. And I think you'd better recognize that problem, that problems of all patients – whether they are pain, anxiety, phobias, insomnia – every one of those problems is a painful thing subjectively to that patient, only you spell the pain sometimes as p-a-i-n, sometimes you spell it p-h-o-b-i-a. Now, they're equally hurtful. And therefore, you ought to recognize the common identity of all your patients. And your problem is, first of all, to take this human being and give him some form of comfort." (see Havens, 2003, pp. 117–118).

This comment, so reminiscent of Buddha's insights, set me off on a quest for strategies to understand and alleviate pain of all types – physical, psychological, and emotional. Eventually, this quest also led me to wonder how to best alleviate my own spiritual and emotional pain and thus, as noted earlier, I came back to the study of cosmic consciousness and to the observations and propositions presented in this chapter. Not only do these propositions offer a useful description of the physical, mental, and spiritual suffering created by the conscious mind, they also provide a useful way of thinking about the changes required to alleviate that suffering, including an escape into a cosmic mind. As such, these propositions represent a remarkably useful conceptual tool for present purposes, even though they do not represent an empirically established explanatory model.

People Are Suffering

Proposition # 1. People throughout the world are suffering emotionally, mentally, physically, interpersonally, and/or spiritually.

Virtually every problem presented to physicians, pastors, counselors, or psychotherapists is a form of suffering. That suffering may stem from a painful physical injury, an inflammatory infection, or from the pain caused by a loss, inadequacy, frustration, stress, failure, deprivation, loneliness, boredom, confusion, or fear. It does not matter what the source of the pain is. The suffering that people experience from each type of painful event can be equally overwhelming and debilitating.

Irritating or painful events cannot be avoided. Let's face it – life is full of various sources of pain. There are injuries, illnesses, irritations, disappointments, hassles, annoyances, and sorrows at every turn, or at least it often seems that way. We get burned, bruised, broken, and infected. Our teeth decay, our joints deteriorate, our muscles get injured, and our bodies send a variety of aches and pains our way, often continuously. But physical pains are just the tip of the iceberg.

The people we like or love abandon and betray us, sometimes they even die. We can end up feeling isolated, completely alone or continuously grieving our losses. Meanwhile, the people we do not like or who are mean and dangerous refuse to go away and leave us alone. They harass us, lie to us, take advantage of us, steal from us, and engage in behaviors we find abhorrent. Or they simply look different, dress differently, behave differently, refuse to believe the truths we accept without question, refuse to accept our God as the only God, refuse to obey our rules, vote for the wrong person, and challenge our reality at every turn and in every way imaginable.

To make matters worse, we often find ourselves not even liking our selves. We do things that we know we ought to not be doing and do not do things that we know we "should". Will power often fails us, firm decisions made in the evening fade away with the sunrise, and good intentions melt into oblivion. We tell lies, take unnecessary risks, break promises, and engage in behaviors that we try to keep hidden from others at all costs. We never have enough time to do everything we think has to be done, much less time to do what we want to do. And no matter how hard we try, we can never do everything well enough or accomplish as much as we intended. There are things left undone, things left unsaid, and things we simply do not have the skills, abilities, or energy to do. And the more we think about things this way, the more we become our own worst enemy, causing more trials and tribulations for ourselves than others ever do.

Meanwhile, it does not matter how hard we work, how much we learn, or how much we earn; it is never enough to satisfy. No matter how many things we know or have, there are always other things we want, something else we believe we need in order to be truly happy. We do not have enough money to buy everything we want or enough to feel financially safe and secure. We do not have enough answers to feel wise and informed. We never quite understand what is going on or why things happen the way they do. Life often just seems overwhelmingly complex, out of control, and completely unpredictable, and we think that is a very bad thing.

Another major source of our ongoing discontent and suffering is that things are always changing all around us. Try as we might, nothing stays the same. Human error, natural disasters, theft, and the mere passage of time eat away at everything we care about. Just when all of the elements of life are exactly the way we want them to be, events conspire to destroy or rearrange it all. Your new car gets scratched or dented, your new house develops cracks in the ceiling, your computer hard drive crashes, your dog gets sick, your child gets arrested for underage drinking, your company declares bankruptcy, your spouse runs off with the neighbor, and your back develops muscle spasms. And then, of course, no matter what you do or how hard you try to ignore it, you are getting older and older and eventually you will die.

The list of potential sources of discord and dismay goes on and on, ranging from the sublime to the ridiculous. Traumas, illness, abuse, droughts, floods, poverty, deprivation, discrimination, riots, wars, pestilence, plagues, too little serotonin, too much adrenalin, not enough friends, no respect, bad hair, baldness, flabbiness, unemployment, boredom, ennui, and a missed putt, all are causing someone somewhere to suffer.

Life is full of potential sources of pain. But do we have to suffer because of them? No, we do not!

Suffering is Created by Judgmental Ideas

Proposition # 2. People are suffering primarily because their ordinary way of looking at or thinking about themselves, their experiences, and the world around them is limited, distorted, biased, prejudiced, and judgmental.

This is not a new or original concept at all. Aside from Buddha, who presented a version of this concept as one of his Noble Truths in the sixth century BCE, numerous philosophers and thinkers throughout the ages have reached a similar conclusion. For example, Epictetus, the first-century Roman philosopher, wrote, "What disturbs men's minds is not events but their judgment on events." Similarly, in 1600, Shakespeare gave Hamlet the line, "… for there is nothing either good or bad, but thinking makes it so." (Act 2, Scene 2). Thus, the notion that life events are disturbing and uncomfortable because of the way people think about them is a familiar concept indeed.

Life seems to be inescapably full of painful events, or at least it is full of events that we judge to be highly unpleasant or even excruciating. But pain, like pleasure, is just another sensation. Whether or not we experience that sensation as disturbing, and suffer from it as a result, depends on how we look at it, how we react to it, and, thus, how we feel about it.

Physical pain is nature's way of announcing that something in the body is not working smoothly or properly. Pain is an alarm, a neural response to a situation that may need attention for one reason or another. Pain tells us when something is out of joint, broken, injured, missing, or just not the way it was originally designed to be. In that sense, pain is quite useful.

Actually, pain is so useful that people who are born without pain sensors tend to have very short life spans because they have no way of knowing when something harmful is happening to them. They often end up with broken bones, infected scrapes, serious bruises, and cuts that have gone unnoticed and thus untreated. They injure themselves frequently without knowing it and at the same time they fail to learn how to avoid such injuries in the future. Physical pain, in other words, is a highly useful sensation, an inherent and necessary part of staying alive.

But the actual sensations associated with physical pain are not always inherently unpleasant or uncomfortable. Pain does not necessarily produce suffering. "Painful" sensations can be jarringly intense and still be quite pleasurable, as anyone who engages in erotic sadomasochistic activities will attest.

Suffering, on the other hand, is what people experience when they are disturbed by the existence of a sensation of pain and vehemently want that sensation to go away. Suffering is the result of a judgmental reaction, a conscious or cognitive response to a "painful" sensation and to the thing causing that sensation. Suffering is the result of labeling and rebelling against the pain and its cause. It is a fear of it, a hatred of it, a rejection of it, a fighting against it, a desire for it to not be there. Unfortunately, when any source of pain, whether a chronic physical pain or an emotional pain or a psychological pain, is viewed as terrible, evil, malevolent, dangerous, or terrifying, the end result is suffering. Painful events cannot be avoided but, as we shall see, judgmental concepts and the suffering they create can be avoided.

Physical suffering results from the belief that a particular sensation is an indication that something bad or horrible is happening to the body. That is what those sensations normally mean. Like the jarring cry of a newborn infant, painful sensations are designed to capture our attention NOW so that we will leap into action to quickly eliminate their source. When such sensations continue on and on, we "know" that more and more damage is being done and so we suffer a lot as a result. But when we know that a sensation does not mean that there is anything wrong, we can relax and ignore it if we wish.

As long as surgical patients are certain that the surgeon is not attacking them or about to kill them, they can relax and ignore what is going on. Similarly, as long as a person is certain that the physical sensation from an injured nerve is meaningless and not an indication of something that requires additional attention, suffering is not necessary. Such meaningless sensations can be examined with a disinterested detachment and then they can be ignored entirely. This is exactly what my clients suffering from phantom limb pain and other forms of chronic and acute pain learn to do.

Hypnosis is an effective way to help people adopt a detached and calm mental attitude. While in a trance state a sensation can be examined from a distance, evaluated as irrelevant, and dismissed from consideration. Absolute faith in a dentist or surgeon has a similar effect. People can be persuaded to ignore the sensations from a surgical or dental procedure if they can be convinced that it is safe to do so. Chronic headache pain can be eliminated once the person becomes convinced that it does not mean that there is a tumor in her head or a blood vessel about to burst there. Once a person stops misinterpreting, rejecting, or reacting emotionally to a sensation, that sensation can stop being a source of suffering.

Even when a pain is associated with ongoing damage that may eventually lead to death, those sensations do not necessarily have to result in severe suffering. To paraphrase an idea repeated frequently by Kay Thompson, DDS, past president of the American Society of Clinical Hypnosis, once everything that can be done has been done, there is no particular reason to fight with or even to experience those sensations any longer. There is no reason to pay attention to them because there is nothing that can be done to alleviate or change the situation causing them. They are irrelevant at that point. When hypnosis is used to convey this idea effectively and completely, the suffering usually diminishes and the pain sensation itself may even disappear entirely from awareness. There simply is no point in paying attention to something that is meaningless, much less in being bothered by it.

But most sources of human suffering are not physiologically based and are not innately painful, much less a legitimate basis for suffering. They are painful merely because they indicate that things are not the way we *want* them to be or think they *ought* to be. They are events that are inconsistent with our idea of peace and harmony. Like much contemporary music or music from other cultures, they seem discordant and jarring to our sense of a desirable reality. They are painful or cause suffering merely because they are not consistent with the way we want the world to be, the way we believe it should be.

Unfortunately, many of our ideas, values, beliefs, and attitudes about the way reality "should be" bear little or no relationship to the way reality is. If anything, reality seems to consistently refuse to conform to our preferences and paradigms. Instead of feeling embraced by, in tune with, and safe in the world, therefore, we often end up feeling at odds with and attacked by the natural course of everyday events, by the actions and comments of our friends and lovers, and even by our own thoughts, impulses, and physical desires. When the world fails to behave the way we want it to or expect it to, the universe seems harsh, coldly uncaring, or downright mean. We can end up feeling frustrated and vulnerable, unable to find more than a momentary spasm of inner peace or a fleeting glimpse of joy.

And all of this suffering occurs simply because we believe that we know the way things *ought* to be in spite of the fact that we are continually reminded that they are not that way. We believe that we know what perfection is, and the world refuses to comply with our bizarre notions. We believe that our own personal conscious view of reality is the "right" one, the only good and true one, but our perception of reality continues to produce frustration and suffering because reality refuses to conform to our limited or constricted idea of the way the real world ought to behave.

No wonder many people suffer from debilitating bouts of depression and paralyzing frenzies of anxiety. It is even a bit surprising that more of us are not more seriously disturbed than we are. Luckily, there is a way out; there is a way to avoid all of this suffering and to experience joy instead. If suffering is primarily the result of the judgmental biases and beliefs about the way things should be, then the way to reduce suffering seems pretty obvious.

To Eliminate Suffering, Eliminate Judgmental Ideas

Proposition # 3. To eliminate suffering, people must overcome the limited, biased, and prejudiced expectations, wants, hopes, and desires of their ordinary way of thinking about things.

This proposition is nothing more than a logical extension of the previous proposition. If suffering is the result of biased or unrealistic ideas about the way things ought to be, then it is obvious that the elimination of suffering requires the elimination of those unrealistic or biased ideas.

In recent decades, cognitive therapists have demonstrated the validity of this proposition in numerous empirically based research studies. When irrational, critical, or pessimistic ideas are challenged and replaced by more optimistic and self-enhancing concepts, people feel better. They experience less psychological or emotional pain (anxiety or depression). This is now essentially an empirically established fact.

Cognitive therapists use various strategies (including interviews, questionnaires and even computerized assessments of reactions to different words and images) to identify consciously and unconsciously held biases, prejudices, beliefs, and attitudes. They then use rational discourse, persuasive arguments, and various assignments or experiential exercises to prove that these beliefs and ideas are self-defeating, irrational, and false. Finally, their patients are encouraged to intentionally interrupt or override those irrational ideas and behaviors and to replace them with more optimistic and self enhancing ones.

As noted above, hypnotherapists have demonstrated the effectiveness of a similar approach with regard to physical pain. Hypnosis can be used to identify and to eliminate irrational beliefs or fears regarding the sources or implications of a particular sensation, even one that seems excruciating. Once a person has been persuaded or hypnotically convinced that a sensation is irrelevant (that it does not mean that the surgeon is going to murder them), then there is no logical reason to pay attention to it and the patient can begin to allow that "painful" sensation to fade into the background or even disappear altogether. Painful depressive notions and disturbing worries can be treated in the same fashion, by using hypnosis to challenge and replace the irrational beliefs and counterproductive attitudes underlying the individual's suffering.

But the procedures presented in this book were designed to do much more than challenge a few irrational beliefs and illogical, counterproductive, or pain-inducing assumptions. The replacement of pessimistic, fearful, or self-critical attitudes and behaviors with more optimistic and accepting ones may, indeed, produce a more comfortable state of mind, but it does not produce the types of quantum transformations in perspective that we are concerned with here. The goal here is not merely to change irrational beliefs and to replace judgmental assumptions; the goal here is to eliminate irrational beliefs and judgmental assumptions altogether.

To Eliminate Judgmental Ideas, Create Cosmic Consciousness

Proposition # 4. During a cosmic or mystical experience, all firmly held judgmental ideas and unconsciously embedded assumptions become irrelevant and immaterial.

Cosmic consciousness experiences do not eliminate judgmental ideas in a step by step application of persuasive logic, ethics, or reason. Instead, the judgmental differentiations and simplistic dichotomies of the conscious mind are simply overwhelmed, buried, or eradicated in a rush of enlightened ecstasy. The all-inclusive, integrative nature of the mystical experience is incompatible with simple-minded dichotomous notions.

Enlightenment involves an unfiltered experience of oneness and integrative perfection. During such an experience, all differentiations, all evaluative judgments, and even all thoughts, whether irrational or rational, optimistic or pessimistic, become momentarily irrelevant and unimportant. They are replaced or overridden for a time by the direct sensory, emotional and cognitive intensity of the mystical experience, e.g., by a direct participation in the cosmos as a unitary essence. Afterwards, many of the most unpleasant, counterproductive, or destructive of these pre-epiphany ideas will seem to be quite meaningless and unimportant and will be eliminated from further consideration. The end result of that process will be a major shift in the person's overall perspective on reality, a change that ultimately will produce a lot less suffering, a lot more understanding, and lot more joy.

The extent of change produced by such experiences must not be underestimated. The consequences of mystical transformations can be pervasive. From the point of view of the person involved, it may be a new beginning, the start of a new life, a new identity, or a new set of values, beliefs, and behaviors. Everything, from basic attitudes to career choices, may suddenly be replaced or morphed into something quite different from what was there before. Some of these changes are obvious to the person, may feel quite intentional, and be easily acknowledged. Others are more subtle and out of the person's range of awareness. These "unconscious", automatic, and essentially irresistible changes are the source of some of the most profound and influential alterations created by cosmic experiences. People change in ways that they may recognize only in hindsight, long after the fact or only after others, who may see these changes immediately, have pointed them out.

Luckily the human brain seems to be particularly well-suited for such massive and pervasive transformations in perspective. Not only is it capable of believing virtually anything, as history amply demonstrates, it also is remarkably malleable or plastic. Santa Claus can be a firm reality one day, and a myth of unbelievable silliness the next. People can and do change their minds on a moment's notice, sometimes because they are faced with irrefutable evidence, sometimes for no discernible reason at all, and sometimes because they have just undergone a shift in awareness of cosmic proportions (see Conway & Siegelman, 1995). The flexibility, modifiability, malleability, or plasticity of our beliefs, thoughts, and attitudes is astonishing, as any cult leader will attest.

No matter what you believe now, you have the unconscious potential to stop believing it and to start believing something else entirely, including exactly the opposite of what you now firmly believe. People can and do believe anything, even things that are completely irrational and utterly unrealistic. What is most impressive to consider, however, is that if people can stop believing anything they believe, then they can stop believing *everything* they believe. This means that to a large extent they have the ability to return to their original state of ignorant bliss, a process I would refer to as a reestablishment of our original condition of "pluripotentiality". And re-entering a state of pluripotentiality, as we shall see in the next section, is comparable in my framework to entering a state of cosmic consciousness.

To Create Cosmic Consciousness, Reestablish Pluripotentiality

Proposition # 5. Cosmic consciousness, enlightenment, mystical aware-ness, or whatever you choose to call it at this point, is the result of a pluripotential state of mind.

Pluripotentiality is a term originally and ordinarily used to describe the capacity of an embryonic stem cell to become any type of cell in the human body. Depending on where it is located within the developing blastocyst, an embryonic stem cell eventu-ally may become a bone, an eye, or even a kidney. Similarly, every normal undifferentiated infant mind is pluripotential in the sense that it has the potential to become virtually anyone, depending on where it is placed.

Initially, every child's mind has the potential to cheerfully adopt almost any idea, attitude, value, or understanding ever adopted by anyone anywhere and to believe it absolutely. No matter where a child is born or what their ancestry or genetic heritage might be, that child is theoretically capable (within reason and given any limits imposed by the rest of that child's physiology) of learning any language, adopting any conceptual system, mastering any knowledge base, or developing any skill set that ever has been used or ever will be used by any ordinary human being anywhere.

Genetic and biological variations play an obvious and powerful role in defining individual differences. Your unique biology played a significant role in determining how you would be per-manently different from your immediate relatives, neighbors, and friends (e.g., taller, shorter, brighter, faster, slower, lighter, darker, more or less reactive physiologically, etc.). But you also have a great deal in common with your neighbors and friends, including language, basic attitudes, fundamental beliefs, and general knowledge. In fact, you may have a lot more in common with the people around you than you would have with your identical twin who had somehow managed to grow up in a different country or a different century. Of all the beliefs, attitudes, languages, preferences, ideas, skills, and interests that you could have developed, the ones that you did develop are the ones that are not only compatible with your neurophysiology but also with the time and place where you were born and with your own unique learning history.

Thus, who you now think you are and what you now believe about yourself and the world around you were defined for you, to a large extent, by the social, cultural, and situational context of your life. You did not become all you could be. You became what you were supposed to be or what you could be given your circumstances and opportunities.

For example, every child is born with the potential to learn how to make every sound that ever has been or ever will be used in any human language. This is an inherent capacity of the human brain. But a child raised in Japan by a Japanese family quickly learns to imitate only the sounds involved in the Japanese language. Eventually, that child's ability to make sounds that belong to other languages will fade and the latent and unused ability to make those other sounds may become lost almost entirely. This is why learning to speak a foreign language later in life can be so frustrating. Sounds that every three-year-old in England can make may seem awkward or even impossible to people who grew up speaking a different language, such as Japanese or Greek. They may never be able to speak that second language without a noticeable accent. Their original linguistic potentialities have been trimmed and constrained into a particular form, much as the original complex potentialities of a young tree are constrained and limited when it is espaliered against a wall.

This same pruning and restraining analogy also applies to the vast range of potential values, attitudes, tastes, and preferences that every child could potentially adopt. Some of them will be emphasized and become firmly embedded while the rest will fade from the

scene to a large extent. Raw fish may become your preferred deli-
cacy if you are raised in one culture but disgust you if you are
raised in another. Roast dog stuffed with fried beetles and live
worms might sound delicious or repulsive depending entirely on
your background.

But this is merely the tip of the iceberg. Every child also has the
potential to learn how to understand any story ever written, to
grasp almost any theoretical concept ever proposed, to believe
anything ever believed, and to imagine anything ever imagined.
Every child has the potential to see and hear every detail of life
anyone has ever noticed, to speak any sentence ever spoken, to
experience anything ever experienced, and to love, hate, or enjoy
every taste, every sound, every image, every smell, every sensation, and every activity ever loved, hated or enjoyed anywhere by
anyone. And every newborn enters the world with the potential to
learn virtually any ability ever learned by anyone, from tight rope
walking to fencing, from dancing to playing poker, from piano
playing to yo-yoing, from making arrowheads to making music.

Over time, a relatively short time actually, the original potential to
learn, believe, or do practically anything is replaced by a specific
set of understandings, abilities, values, and beliefs. The infant's
pluripotentiality is reduced and refined down into a more manageable and useful collection of judgments, labels, critiques, ideas,
and skills. In some cases those beliefs may even include the notion
that all other ideas, beliefs, and values are stupid, wrong, dangerous, sinful, or even evil.

The end result of this process of increasing differentiation and
restricted potentialities is a person with a specific set of beliefs,
values, and abilities that are active on both conscious and unconscious levels. The conscious level contains ideas and abilities that
the person is aware of and can influence rather directly. The
unconscious level contains ideas and abilities that generally exist
and operate outside the range of that individual's awareness or
control. Taken together, these conscious and unconscious frag-
ments of what was originally a broad range of pluripotentiality
coalesce to become a specific and unique person, an identity differentiated from all of the potential identities that person could
have become.

As each child's original pluripotentiality becomes differentiated into specific sets of ideas, beliefs and abilities, the world around that child becomes increasingly differentiated as well, at least from the point of view of the child. What originally seems like an over-whelmingly complex, essentially magical, and largely mysterious universe gradually becomes more and more conceptually manageable as each part is separated from all the others, named, explained, and evaluated. The mind gradually breaks down the universe into its component parts, much as a child takes a watch apart to see what makes it work. Each piece is named, evaluated, and given a place in the general scheme of things. As a result of this process, the universe seems less and less miraculous over time, as well as more and more problematic.

The world begins to seem more problematic because the act of differentiating the parts of the world that are desirable or acceptable from those that are undesirable and unacceptable automatically generates dissatisfaction, as noted above in *Proposition # 2*. This evaluative process leads us to become more and more alienated or separated from the world around us. Our artificial and judgmental differentiations are invaluable strategies for arranging and dealing with reality, but they also are the source of most human suffering.

Luckily, remnants of the mind's original pluripotentiality continue to exist somewhere within the complexities of the brain. Although many of the original possibilities and potentials of each human mind are lost through atrophy (actual physical disappearance of unused neural interconnections) by the time a person reaches adulthood, many others survive. Just as the differentiated cells within the bone marrow of each adult continue to show some degree of pluripotentiality, every individual continues to possess a huge range of unacknowledged abilities, unused potentials, and unexplored possibilities in the background of awareness that are not being expressed or acknowledged but do still exist. They are dormant – unused, overlooked, and ignored – but ready to burst forth if given the opportunity or encouragement to do so.

As a result, the original pluripotentiality and malleability of the human mind can be approximated or even resurrected to some extent. When an intense flash of activity throughout the cerebral circuitry ignites an enlightenment experience, connections that were previously unused or unavailable suddenly burst into being. Instead of the highly differentiated and limited patterns of activity typical of everyday life, the brain erupts into a massive rush of interconnected chatter. All of those potential connections that the person has learned to ignore or suppress suddenly become active or available again. Ideas that were unimaginable suddenly spring to life, perceptions that were unacceptable become engaging and gorgeous, feelings that were forgotten long ago are reborn, and interconnections that were broken merge together once again.

But just as adult stem cells do not have the same degree of pluripotentiality or plasticity as embryonic stem cells, there are limits to the potentiality of the adult human mind. As a result, cosmic consciousness experiences are immersions in a state of mind that is similar to but less flexible, less naïve, and more preprogrammed than the original pluripotential condition. Cosmic consciousness is not the blank, unknowing wonderment of an infant; it is the explosively joyful awareness of an adult. Boundaries tend to weaken and become more ephemeral but they do not disappear altogether. Things that previously seemed to be separate and imperfect suddenly become magically entwined and united into a divinely inspired unity. It is as if all the synaptic connections that ordinarily keep things defined and differentiated from each other suddenly expand into a complex tapestry of interconnections, the knots that separated things from each other suddenly becoming loosely woven together into a cosmic cocoon where everything that used to be separate is now a harmonious whole. Mystical experiences are a reintegration at a higher level of analysis than was possible originally.

For example, when children first start listening to music, they get a general impression of each piece. They hear the overall sound which they may find to be either enjoyable or unendurable. But it is impossible for a novice to explain how that overall sound was made or to fully appreciate the artistry involved in playing it. Only after much learning and training is it possible to identify and monitor each instrument or each voice separately and to hear the way they blend and harmonize with each other. A truly sophisticated appreciation of that overall sound is only possible when all of the individual parts can be identified and then heard in relation to each other. The same might be said of the sounds of a forest at night. A wilderness cacophony only turns into a complex set of important and highly coordinated communications between tree frogs, owls, and crickets after each sound has been tagged or attributed to a separate organism. Apply this same idea to the relationship of everything to everything else and you begin to capture the essence of a mystical understanding. Mystical awareness of universal oneness can occur only after everything already has been differentiated, judged, evaluated, and compared with everything else. The flash of cosmic consciousness puts everything back together again in a way that illuminates the sophisticated and unbelievably beautiful patterns of perfect interrelationship that exist between all of the different parts of everything everywhere.

To Reestablish Pluripotentiality, Turn Everything On At Once

Proposition # 6. Pluripotentiality, aka cosmic consciousness, involves an explosion of neural activity throughout the brain.

Whether the perception of perfection and unity that occurs during a mystical state reflects a genuine quality of the magical perfection of reality or is merely a reflection of the design of the brain itself, or both, is an interesting and debatable question, but not an important one. What is important is that such experiences can happen to virtually anyone. It is likely that every normal human brain has the potential to become open to the absolute wonder of it all, to access a spiritually healing enlightenment experience that seems to lie hidden and dormant within each of us. The paradox is that this experience of complete understanding and appreciation occurs only when all of our previous understandings are momentarily blown away or overridden by a surge of unusually intense sensory and conceptual stimulation.

It is apparent from first hand accounts that the state of mind associated with the occurrence of a mystical enlightenment experience is most definitely not an empty or blank state of mind. The cosmic state is not less intense, less aware, or less full than ordinary consciousness. In fact, just the opposite is the case. Cosmic consciousness involves an explosion of brilliant light, harmonic sounds, electrifying sensations, creative insights, and powerful emotions, all at the same time. Awareness becomes full to overflowing, expansively charged, and orgasmically intense. Cosmic consciousness is an eruption of internal activity, not an elimination of it. And as that eruption occurs, all preconceptions, differentiations, and limiting assumptions are simply swept away, overwhelmed by the intensity. They are not destroyed or erased; they are momentarily overwritten by the enormous volume of new possibilities. They are buried, one might say, like great monuments of the past in a blinding avalanche of pure awareness.

The stars are still up there in the sky during the day, but we do not see them because the sun is so bright. Similarly, the things that we knew, felt, and perceived before a cosmic experience are still there during and after that experience, they are just comparatively irrelevant or insignificant. The unfettered surge or flash of sensation, thought, and emotion that occurs during a cosmic consciousness experience momentarily whites out everything else, like a flash bulb, and leaves the mind in a state of supernova-like activation. Previously learned differentiations, categorizations, and conceptualizations fade into the blazingly brilliant background of an intensely activated and highly undifferentiated state of mind, into a kind of mental *ganzfeld*. Within this brilliantly illuminated state, everything becomes possible and everything becomes one. This "whiteout" state of mind can be thought of as an adult version of every newborn child's mental "pluripotentiality".

Some people are able to intentionally create a mental *ganzfeld* or whiteout state through the art of meditation. For example, Lutz, Greischar, Rawlings, Ricard, and Davidson (2004) demonstrated that an intense focus of attention on a subjective sense of loving compassion by experienced Tibetan meditators produces a dramatic increase in brain activity, a flare of high frequency gamma wave activity (30 to 70 Hz), throughout the entire brain and especially in the frontal lobes of the brain. During this form of meditation the brain literally lights up, radiates exceptionally high levels of high frequency activity throughout. Apparently, after years of practice these Tibetan meditators have learned how to directly ignite the inner warmth associated with the feelings of love, compassion, and oneness.

On the other hand, some people apparently experience a similar disinhibiting and heart warming burst of neural activity for no particular reason at all. Perhaps they are less rigidly differentiated in the first place than most people, and thus more open to such unusual spiritual experiences. Or perhaps they are, as Bucke suggested in 1901, more highly evolved than the rest of us, and thus just naturally more prone to the sudden bursts of high frequency activity involved in these cosmic consciousness or mystical enlightenment events.

The scripts within this text were created primarily for people who are neither lucky enough, nor self-actualized enough, nor disciplined enough to spontaneously experience such intense surges of neural activity on a regular basis. The scripts presented here are examples of attempts to create this mental whiteout by using hypnotically induced visual, auditory, kinesthetic or emotional overloads.

Having spent an entire lifetime learning how to distinguish one thing from another, how to name all of those things, and how to determine their relative value, it is amazing to realize that all of those learned constructs can become irrelevant, null and void, in one extraordinarily intense moment. It also is amazing to realize that when the human brain is freed from the limits imposed by all of those carefully learned labels, judgments, prejudices, biases, and narrow perspectives, it can suddenly perceive the universe and everything or everyone in it as perfectly compatible, completely interconnected, unbearably beautiful, and deeply loved. Apparently, lighting up the brain can and does lighten up both the mind and the spirit.

Chapter 4

The Complexities of the Human Mind

Who amongst thee by taking thought can add one cubit to his stature?
Why then take thee thought for raiment? Consider the lilies of the field,
they neither toil nor sow.
—Jesus Christ, The Sermon on the Mount

The brain processes that we call "the mind" are a much more complex and multifaceted mystery than most people realize. Actually, the mind is not a unitary or unified thing at all. The term is just a conceptually and linguistically convenient convention, a shorthand reference to the multiple levels of awareness, information processing, and ongoing functioning that occur within the human brain. A more accurate portrayal would represent the brain as a multitude of subsystems, or mini-minds, each a relatively separate module interacting with many other modules (see Fodor, 1983), some of which then coalesce to form larger subsystems that behave like hives or flocks of coordinated activity. Each large hive of neural circuits or "society of minds" (Bownds, 1999) functions like a loosely integrated but highly coordinated collection of semi-independent beings, just like a flock of birds migrating from one place to another in a seemingly meandering but generally purposeful and directed manner. Thus, every person can be thought of as having many different flocks of mini-minds operating concurrently, layer upon layer and wave after wave of them in fact.

These multiple components of the mind can be sorted into two main flocks or groups. One of these groups of mini-minds is the verbal group. It is located primarily within the temporal area of the left cerebral hemisphere of the brain where it generates language and the primary product of that language – the conscious mind or Self. The other group consists of all of the rest of the mini-minds operating throughout the remainder of the brain. Because these mini-minds exist largely outside the awareness or immediate control of the conscious mind, they are referred to collectively as the "unconscious mind".

This bifurcated view of mental activity is not terribly important for an understanding of cosmic consciousness itself, which involves a transformation of the mind as whole (i.e. of both the conscious and the unconscious levels of functioning at the same time). However, this dualistic construct is a fundamental component of the approach to hypnosis used in the scripts presented Section II of this text. Those hypnotic scripts rest firmly on the proposition that hypnosis involves a quieting or bypassing of the conscious mind or Self so that the abilities and capacities of the unconscious mind can be redirected and used in new or unexpected ways. Thus, before I can attempt to describe the hypnotic process, as I intend to do in the next chapter, I must first briefly introduce the conscious and unconscious realms of the mind.

What is the Conscious Mind?

Although the flock of mini-minds that we each identify with and call "Me" – the conscious mind – dominates everyday awareness and experience, it actually merits very little time or attention in this discussion. The conscious mind is an over-active verbal chatterbox. It generates the myth of "Me" and then spends its time narrating and critiquing the life story of "Me". It also generates all of the unwarranted expectations and catastrophic interpretations that underlie most human suffering, such as those discussed in the previous chapter. It is a critical commentator, an analytic orator, and a judgmental worrier. Although it is the part of the mind with which we are all most comfortable and familiar, it represents only a very small part of all of the ongoing activities and abilities of the human mind/brain, essentially only those activities that occur within the neurons in the verbal centers of the left side of the cerebral cortex.

The verbal conscious mind can notice and talk about things that the other parts of the brain are experiencing, it can babble on to itself *ad infinitum* about almost anything, and it can issue verbal commands that certain non-conscious parts of the brain may or may not obey depending on the situation, but that is about all it actually can do. Everything else, everything other than these language-based cognitive functions, are carried out within the "unconscious" realms of the brain.

Imagine that the mind is a country organized into autonomous states, with each state subdivided into counties and then further subdivided into townships, cities, and neighborhoods, each neighborhood full of different businesses and/or industries and every locale led by a local government, with everything interconnected by rail, roads, and rivers. All of this activity is presided over by a national government – the conscious mind – which makes a lot of speeches and likes to make up rule after rule about what people are supposed to do, but actually has very little power or direct control over what goes on throughout the country from day to day. About the only thing it really can do is toot its own horn, try to persuade the country as a whole to send it money, have meetings with the so-called "leaders" of other countries, and get into wars with them. What happens throughout the country from day to day is much more heavily influenced by state or local businesses and authorities.

As this analogy suggests, the conscious mind could not and would not exist without the support and cooperation of the more productive parts and more widespread parts of the mind, the parts that we are going to call the "unconscious" mind. The conscious mind is a relatively limited, rule-driven, and essentially impotent linguist. It is a useful but narrow-minded, egocentric, and somewhat incompetent bureaucrat. It is partially isolated from and ignorant of the rest of the brain. Even though it thinks that it is the only mind around and that it is totally in charge of all thoughts, actions, and reactions, this is hardly the case. In spite of its inflated sense of self importance and its continuous issuance of orders or directives, the fact is that it, like the federal government, would be in big trouble if it could not rely on the cooperation, autonomous actions, and supportive services of the rest of the system (the unconscious parts) for help in almost every area of life.

What is the Unconscious Mind?

The term "unconscious mind" is potentially even more misleading than the term "mind". For this reason, Prince (1975) sometimes referred to it the "co-conscious self" and I once referred to it as the "unconditioned other" (Havens, 1981). Unfortunately, neither of these alternatives has caught on and so I have chosen to use the more familiar term "unconscious" throughout this text. It is important, however, to avoid the many erroneous connotations commonly associated with this term.

For example, the "unconscious mind" referred to in this text is not unconscious, in the sense of being unresponsive or oblivious like a boxer who has been knocked out. The unconscious mind is only "unconscious" from the conscious mind's point of view! If any-thing, the "unconscious" mind being described here is much more aware of and responsive to internal and external stimuli than the conscious mind. The unconscious keeps track of surrounding events that the conscious mind ignores and often responds to those events without the conscious mind even being aware of it. While the verbally overactive conscious mind is engaged in one conversation at a time, the unconscious mind can actively monitor the other conversations going on in the room and immediately notify the conscious mind if someone across the room says some-thing of personal relevance. This is why you immediately notice when someone mentions your name no matter how noisy the party.

The unconscious also can notice and respond to internal events while the conscious mind does something else entirely. It can notice and scratch an itch while your conscious mind is talking on the phone or take a drink and smooth your hair while your con-scious mind is engrossed in a good book. The unconscious is not only awake, alert, and aware, it is aware of things that otherwise would tend to go unnoticed or ignored by the conscious mind and it actively responds to them.

Another possible source of confusion about the term "unconscious mind" is the meaning that Freud and his followers imposed on it over a century ago. Freud described the unconscious mind as the dank repository of our most basic instincts and the antisocial source of most human conflicts and suffering. His theory proposed that people are basically evil and that this evil resides in the unconscious mind. We now know that the unconscious is, instead, a sophisticated and objective observer of the world as well as a brilliant, skilled, and dedicated helpmate of the conscious mind. It seeks out pleasure, tries to avoid pain, and uses its enormous storehouse of learned responses, hidden potentials, and sophisticated observations to improve all aspects of that individual's life, at least it will if it is allowed to do so. Rather than something to be feared and suppressed, the unconscious is a potential source of love, joy, and competence to be revered and used freely and fully.

The unconscious mind is fundamentally objective and unbiased. Whereas the perceptions of the conscious mind are distorted and filtered through the lenses of prejudicial expectations and biased beliefs, the experiences of the unconscious mind tend to be rather direct or unfiltered, like those of a child. Not being heavily language based or language driven, the unconscious has few erroneous beliefs, vested interests, or hidden agendas that might distort and invalidate its observations. Thus, the information it collects is detailed, catalogued in a relatively detached manner, and not over-interpreted. For the most part, what it sees is what it sees.

Finally, and most importantly, it must be emphasized that the unconscious mind, like the mind itself, is not a unitary thing. It consists of multiple layers of mini-minds, some working alone, others working in concert, and some even working against all of the others, with each layer having duties and purposes different from the others.

The most autonomous and most primitive layers of the unconscious are in charge of the physiological machinery of the body. They can be thought of as invaluable remnants of our primordial past. They monitor and control basic physiological processes such as heart rate, blood pressure, digestion, and cell growth.

The somewhat higher and more "reptilian" levels of the unconscious mind are responsible for sexual and emotional responses. These are directly tied to hormonal processes and, as such, they can have powerful effects on the behavior of the individual.

The evolutionarily newer and more conceptually sophisticated levels of the unconscious mind are responsible for scanning the environment and deciphering all incoming information, for integrating perceptual experiences, for mastering complex physical skills, and for remembering all of this learning for later use. These uppermost layers also are the source of creative intuition, integrative perception, aesthetic appreciation, invention, empathy, insight, and imagination.

The conscious mind receives the insights, physical skills, intuitions, and imaginative concepts of the unconscious spontaneously – as if by magic. Each unconscious component springs into action as needed, from out of the blue, providing an enormous variety of response tendencies and many different forms of information. These gifts can make life much easier, but they also can make life confusing and complicated if the conscious mind does not know how and when to use them effectively. To work well, the mind needs to work as a coordinated package, with the conscious and unconscious components operating together, like a team, each free to do what it does best. Unfortunately, the relationship between them is not always this harmonious or productive.

The Conscious/Unconscious Relationship

The unconscious mind plays an inordinately large, though often unacknowledged, role in everyday life. Thanks to the unconscious we do not have to be consciously aware of or in charge of most of what we say, think, do, or feel. The unconscious handles a majority of the demands of everyday life, thus freeing up the conscious mind for its own linguistic, philosophical, analytic pursuits. This, it turns out, is a very good thing, because if the conscious mind had to be in charge of everything all the time, everyone would have a hard time surviving, much less getting out of bed and stumbling into the bathroom in the morning. It is easy to demonstrate this point – just try taking charge of your breathing for the next few hours.

It is possible to control your breathing, of course, everyone can do it. But it is almost impossible to control your breathing as well as your unconscious does it, and it is essentially impossible to do it for very long without getting distracted and forgetting to pay attention to it at all. Changing the frequency and depth of each inhalation and exhalation in response to the specific oxygen requirements of the body requires constant vigilance and full attention. If at the same time you also had to be in charge of all other biological processes, such as blood pressure, skin conductivity, hormone balances, digestion, and heart rate, you would be dead within minutes, if not seconds. It is just too much for the conscious mind to juggle.

For the most part, these quiet biological events are ignored or overlooked entirely by the conscious mind while the unconscious components of the brain manage them with the sophistication of an orchestra conductor. Biofeedback technology can magnify these events and, thus, push them into the realm of conscious awareness which then makes it possible for the conscious mind to learn how to modify or direct them. Heart rate, breathing rate, muscle tension, and blood pressure all can be altered intentionally in this manner. Instead of depending on technology to amplify these subtle events enough to make them consciously perceptible, it also is possible to ignore everything else and to pay such close attention to them that they become noticeable. The yogis of India provide clear evidence that with practice and discipline it is possible to consciously recognize and influence things like blood pressure, metabolic rate, and heart rate. Luckily, however, most of the time it is perfectly okay, or even preferable, to ignore such biological processes and to allow the unconscious to take care of them without any conscious participation at all.

Just as we rely on various non-Self or unconscious sections of the brain to manage and coordinate our basic vegetative functions, we also depend on the unconscious parts of the brain to manage the basic processes underlying perception, memory, movement, learning, and even creative invention. For example, some non-conscious modules of the brain process color while others record shape and movement, others modify the convergence of the eyes, and others change the position of the lens in the eye to maintain a clear visual image, all of which is then integrated into a coherent moving picture of the scene in another unconscious module. Similar unconscious modules manage and integrate the various elements of hearing, taste, touch and smell, and eventually all of this is automatically and unconsciously compressed into a coherent version of the world around us.

In addition, the unconscious manages memory and learning for us. It remembers names, dates, telephone numbers, information heard on the radio, commercials from TV, people met at a party, a favorite song, the content of a footnote in a book read years before, and the taste of your first real kiss. It is a repository of remembered experiences and information, a storehouse of knowledge gained via repetition and impression. It also is an obedient and efficient search engine which can scan this repository and find whatever fact or memory is called for at that particular moment. How many times have you tried unsuccessfully to remember a name and said to yourself or someone else, "Oh well, it will come to me." And then it did. A few minutes later and "poof", there it was. The unconscious can be quite helpful that way.

Unconscious subroutines also are in charge of the physical coordination involved in behaviors such as standing, walking, and talking. Such over-learned responses can and often do occur without any conscious intent or monitoring, which is why people can walk, talk, and chew gum at the same time. Even complex behaviors such as driving a car, lighting and smoking a cigar, buttoning or unbuttoning a shirt, and carrying on a conversation, or highly sophisticated skills such as hitting a tennis ball or a golf ball, are monitored and carried out by non-conscious parts of the brain. Once these complex physical tasks are mastered to the point of automaticity, they are stored and controlled in the unconscious realm.

In fact, the "unconscious" modules of the brain are so much better at coordinating physical movement that once people master a skill, they can then perform that skill much more perfectly when they simply relax, observe, and passively allow the unconscious components of the brain to do whatever needs to be done without any conscious criticism or interference. This is also true of many cognitive skills. Once the unconscious learns how to do so, it can read for us, understand the meaning of words for us, decide which meaning of a word best suits the context, and solve math problems for us. These unconscious servants are a remarkable luxury inherited by everyone. They pamper, indulge, entertain, and move the conscious mind from place to place while also keeping it alive, reminding it of its itinerary, and providing it with a decent script to follow most of the time.

It may be relatively easy for you to accept and to acknowledge that the unconscious parts of your brain are responsible for carrying out basic vegetative, performance, and cognitive activities for you. It also may be reassuring to know that you can rely on the unconscious components of the brain to automatically and efficiently carry out many higher order memory and problem solving functions for you. After all, without such unconscious subroutines it would be impossible to do the kind of multitasking that we so often see in our offices and on our highways, no one would ever sink a 50 foot putt, and reading a stop sign would be as difficult today as it was when you first began learning how to read. On the other hand, it may be more difficult to accept the fact that your unconscious mind is busy influencing major life choices such as who to marry and what job to accept. Trusting the unconscious to make such decisions may be advisable, but it is difficult for most people to do.

Trusting and working cooperatively with the unconscious allows people to become incredibly skillful, to enter a zone of perfection, to go with the flow, and to experience peak performances (Csikszentmihalyi, 1990). When the conscious mind provides a clear goal, stays passively focused on the relevant perceptions, and trusts the unconscious to respond in the best way possible, skills become mastered and performances become masterful. The archer becomes the arrow soaring to the bull's-eye, the pitcher feels the ball hitting the catcher's mitt, and the dancer moves with the effortless grace of a gazelle. When the conscious and unconscious minds operate together cooperatively, in tandem like a team of horses, things go very well. When they do not, however, problems can arise.

People do not always trust or rely upon their unconscious and may even interfere with it at times. When the conscious mind does not trust the unconscious people can become incredibly awkward and even downright incompetent. It is easy to walk along a one-foot wide beam resting on the ground, but put that beam 100 feet in the air and suddenly people become quite awkward, perhaps unable to move. If you want to watch someone slip and fall on the ice, just persuade that person to be really careful while walking across it. The interference caused by conscious caution and hesitation is almost guaranteed to make walking an awkward, tentative, and uncoordinated process and it will often produce an unintentional pratfall.

Not trusting the unconscious, not working cooperatively with it, can create problems in most areas of life. When allowed to do so, the unconscious can do most things very competently; even make those very personal decisions such as who to marry, what clothes to buy, what job to take, and where to live. In fact, assessing complex situations and making sophisticated decisions about them is one of the things it is supposed to do. When it is sidetracked by irrelevant conscious concerns or considerations and interfered with by a conscious redirection of perception or attention, however, then life itself can become awkward and difficult.

When the conscious mind ignores information or suggestions from the unconscious, when it purposefully overlooks the subtle unconscious messages we call "intuition", it risks making decisions based on its own biased or prejudicial attitudes alone. How many people ignore the nagging doubts of the unconscious mind and end up getting married to the wrong person for the wrong reasons? A certain hair color, body type, or turn of phrase may appeal to the prejudices of the conscious mind, but the unconscious mind will notice mannerisms and voice inflections that lead it to silently implore, "Run away and run away fast!" Similarly, people often decide to buy or do things in spite of an underlying feeling that what they are about to do is stupid, wrong, or even dangerous, only to regret that decision later on. The unconscious may be incredibly wise and well informed, but people will still tend to ignore it when its recommendations conflict with their judgmental conscious beliefs and values.

The tendency to rely heavily, and usually inappropriately, on conscious understandings and to deny or overlook conflicting unconscious input is the subject of the quotation presented at the beginning of this chapter wherein Christ wonders why people insist on cloaking themselves in thought instead of allowing themselves to rely upon their natural sources of "intuitive" intelligence.

The book *Blink* by Malcolm Gladwell (2005) provides a readable summary of the current literature on a similar subject and raises essentially the same issue. Why, he wonders, do we so often ignore or deny our "unconscious" sources of understanding, insight, and skillful response? Why does the conscious Self so often refuse to pay attention to or trust the unconscious mind? Why does it continue to make unnecessary blunders and to deny or overlook abilities that could make life so much simpler?

There are many possible answers to this question. Ignorance, lack of training, improper training, and an unwillingness of the conscious mind/Self to admit its own limitations are a few of the more common factors. But perhaps the most interesting and detrimental disconnection between the conscious and the unconscious occurs in response to the amazing abilities that people demonstrate during hypnosis. During hypnosis people are able to experience and do things that seem unbelievable and even impossible to most of us. The abilities and potentials demonstrated by hypnotized subjects are so far beyond our ordinary understanding of normal human capacities that they seem unreal or even supernatural. As far as the conscious mind of most people is concerned, such abilities do not even exist, they are taboo, banned.

Taboo Abilities and Hypnotic Responses

The mind contains a hidden library of banned books, a museum of unusual oddities and unbelievable abilities, a vast storehouse of weirdness, a huge collection of overlooked potentials and unacknowledged possibilities, a deeply buried source of unimaginable wisdom, insight, and tolerance that typically goes overlooked and ignored. These abilities seem so unbelievably and disturbingly powerful and unexplainable that they are locked away from conscious consideration altogether. This is where we hide what we knew before we were taught a language, social etiquette, or social taboos. This is where we keep what we knew before we became ignorant and where we store what we have learned but are still not allowed to know.

When it comes to these seemingly unusual, unacceptable, and apparently frightening abilities, the boundary between the conscious and unconscious is closed and closely guarded for most people most of the time. The suspicions and superstitions of the conscious mind absolutely ban a free expression of or acknowledgement of these particular forms of information and ability.

The abilities and potentials referred to here are consciously denied, ignored, and overlooked simply because they contradict our contrived and limited beliefs about ourselves. The problem is that we know much more than we are supposed to know, we notice things that we do not believe we can notice, and we can do things that we do not believe we can do. We do all of these things all of the time, they are normal and natural and easily detectable, but they are so far outside the realm of our beliefs about ourselves that we do not recognize them. People constantly modify and ignore sensations, hallucinate, purposefully forget things, remember things they did not know they knew, and receive subtle unintentional messages from others. They just do not consciously recognize such incidents.

Rather than accept that such things are perfectly normal and expand our definition of ourselves, we invent supernatural explanations, such as telepathy, to explain things like the perception and interpretation of incredibly subtle cues from others and we invent unusual states of mind, such as hypnosis, to explain and excuse many of our other remarkable abilities, such as the ability to ignore pain or to experience visual and auditory hallucinations. These taboo capacities are like having a collection of unexpectedly powerful genies in a bottle. They provide a reservoir of potentials and capacities that are dangerously powerful, intriguingly mysterious, and incredibly valuable all at the same time. The abilities they provide are too real to ignore, but too contrary to everyday notions of normal human capacities to be accepted as normal. Instead of expanding the common notion of normal, which would seem to be the reasonable thing to do under those circumstances, it apparently is simpler or easier to view these abilities as abnormal or even paranormal.

The ability that seems to be especially problematic, and the one that may underlie all of the others, is the ability to imagine something so vividly that it is experienced as being real. Children can imagine virtually anything. This conceptual flexibility is a major component of their original pluripotentiality. They can conjure up images of things that they have never seen and they can imagine themselves experiencing or doing things that they never would or could do in real life.

Furthermore, the things that children experience only in imagination are almost as important to their ongoing development as the things that they actually do experience. Sometimes they are even more important. If you cannot imagine yourself doing something, you may not even try to do it. Why bother. On the other hand, once you do imagine yourself doing something then you may almost feel compelled to do it. People can be watching television and suddenly begin imagining themselves eating ice cream. They can imagine the taste of the very ice cream they currently have in the refrigerator and within a few minutes wonder why they are standing there eating that pint of ice cream. And if for some reason you imagine a friend or lover doing something that you either do not like at all or that you like very much, that imagined event may change your entire attitude about the person.

Imagination is a much more powerful tool than most people imagine. It is virtually unlimited in scope, which is exactly why the conscious mind has trouble with it and shoves it into the unconscious realm where it then goes overlooked and is frequently misused. Because the human brain can imagine unrealistic, unpleasant, or downright disturbing things just as easily as it can imagine pleasant things, it is not surprising that we often scare ourselves with our own imagination and subsequently learn to shy away from it. Dark shadows in the corner of a dark bedroom can easily become a hideous murderer preparing to viciously tear us limb from limb. Random sounds can become a demonic ghost walking down the hall. The view from the thirtieth floor of a skyscraper can produce an immediate and stomach turning image of plunging toward the ground.

No wonder people often pull away from and eventually lose touch altogether with their own imaginative abilities. And when a child uses their imagination to create a playmate for company, parents can become uncomfortable and may even insist that this imagined friend must disappear. If their insistence does not work, they may begin to consider either psychotherapy or even an exorcism.

Getting lost in imagined realities is simply not done. Past a certain young age, it becomes unseemly and unacceptable.

The suppression of imagination for any reason is a tremendous loss because imagination is such a direct route into so many amazing abilities, experiences, and potentials. In fact, I maintain that imagination is the basis for, among many other things, all hypnotic responses. Without it, neither hypnosis nor many of the phenomena associated with hypnosis would exist. This view of hypnosis is somewhat atypical and, as such, it requires additional discussion and explanation. That is the purpose of the next chapter.

Chapter 5

Hypnotic Events

*Trance is a focusing on one thing ... dropping all the peripheral foci
and narrowing it down to one focus.*
—Milton H. Erickson, in Erickson & Rossi, 1979, p. 369

The basic goal of all of the hypnotic procedures presented in this text is quite simple ... to help people learn how to experience a trance state and then use that trance state to experience one or more of the components of a cosmic consciousness episode. To help yourself or others accomplish this you will need to have a working understanding of the hypnotic process – at least a minimalistic notion of what it is and how to use it. Accordingly, this chapter contains a simplistic but pragmatically useful description of hypnotic abilities, hypnotic trance, and the steps involved in a typical hypnotic process.

The discussion of hypnosis presented here is admittedly idiosyncratic. It represents my own particular point of view and is not meant to be representative of the attitudes commonly held by others in the field. On the other hand, I must confess that there is no commonly accepted understanding of hypnosis by others in the field. Instead, there is an ongoing debate about the nature and even the existence of hypnosis. For example, Division 30 of the American Psychological Association recently published its two-paragraph definition of hypnosis (Green, Barabasz, Barrett, and Montgomery, 2005). This definition was instantly challenged and dissected within the same journal (Nash, 2005 and Christensen, 2005) and subsequently in a series of articles published in the *American Journal of Clinical Hypnosis*, Vol. 48, No. 2–3, October 2005/January 2006. Whether or not the hypnotic approach used in my scripts meets the definition of hypnosis preferred by one camp or another within the field, I still believe that it is one of the most pragmatically useful points of view around.

The Nature and Source of Hypnotic Responses

As noted in the previous chapter, I maintain that hypnotic responses are nothing more than abilities and potentials that everyone has and that everyone uses and relies on every day, but are not supposed to have and do not believe they have. Within this conceptualization, the split between what you believe you are and all of the potentials and abilities that you actually are is the reason that we even have something called hypnosis. About 150 years ago people invented a magical state of mind that they eventually called "hypnotic trance" to explain things that they could do (hallucinate, for example) that they did not believe that they could or should be able to do in an ordinary state of mind. As a result we now have the belief that hypnosis somehow endows a person with amazing abilities that did not exist beforehand and would not exist were it not for this special state of mind. From my point of view, of course, this is a silly belief.

The ability to hallucinate seems bizarre or even scary to most people, as does the ability to modify various physiological responses or to endure major surgery with no apparent suffering. In our culture, the only occasions when it is at all acceptable to allow such things to occur is during an intense religious experience, during a crisis situation, under the influence of mind-altering drugs, and, within the last 150 years at least, during a hypnotic trance. Under these various "trance-inducing" or mind-altering circumstances it is acceptable for people to do or to experience things that we ordinarily think of as "extraordinary", such as seeing visions, hearing voices, engaging in automatic movement or speech, experiencing spontaneous healings, or demonstrating extraordinary feats of memory, pain tolerance, and strength. But the simple fact is that we all demonstrate minor versions of these same phenomena all the time. We ignore uncomfortable sensations, for example, and we think we heard the phone ringing when it did not. We also experience automatic movement whenever we reach out and catch something thrown to us without thinking about it, we sometimes duck away from something that was not really there, and we may even unexpectedly remember a long-forgotten detail from childhood.

If you know that you can do these things without being in a trance, or even do them all the time, you might want to keep that bit of information to yourself. Such abilities are still viewed as *pro forma* evidence of either insanity or demon possession by many people. If you doubt this, tell a few friends that there is a six-foot tall rabbit called Harvey following you around and see what reaction you get. Young children can have imaginary playmates, but adults are not supposed to do that any more, even if it is a wonderfully entertaining use of a perfectly good "hypnotic" ability. Similarly, if you think that you hear someone calling your name when you are in the shower, and you turn off the shower to check, and there was no one there, better to keep it to yourself. Unless you are in a trance, which offers a good, socially acceptable excuse to experience such "non-normal" and unacceptable things, then you are supposed to ignore or even deny them.

Hypnosis, therefore, is a ritual that gives people an excuse and an opportunity to use abilities and potentials that otherwise must be kept under wraps, hidden in the background, or relegated to the realm that I am calling "the unconscious mind" in this text. Within this definition "hypnotic" responses are nothing more than abilities and potentials that ordinarily go overlooked, denied, suppressed, unused, or even misused. Hypnotic inductions do not mystically create new abilities. Hypnotic responses are simply examples of abilities that we do not believe we have or are not comfortable allowing ourselves to experience, except under those circumstances that we have agreed to call a "hypnotic trance". Nonetheless, they are abilities we use every day.

One of the most impressive of these "hypnotic" abilities is the wonderful ability to eliminate the suffering that can be created by various sources of physical and emotional pain. People are amazed when confronted by the ability of a hypnotized patient to undergo major surgery, even amputation of a leg or an arm, with no anesthesia at all and no apparent discomfort. But this is the same ability non-hypnotized individuals demonstrate when they ignore the uncomfortable sensation of sitting on a hard bench for hours while listening to a fascinating speech or when soccer players immediately forget about that whack in the shins even though the injury is still there. Such incidents are perfectly good examples of phenomena usually restricted to a hypnotic trance, but they are not recognized as such.

People are amused and impressed when they see a hypnotized subject hallucinate and play with an object that is not really there or fail to see something that is right in front of their face. They may be equally impressed when a hypnotized subject recites a poem memorized in the fifth grade or remembers the names of all second grade classmates and where each one sat in the classroom. And they are often very surprised when a hypnotized subject stays standing in the same awkward position for much longer than seems humanly possible or develops a red mark when touched with a supposedly hot (but actually cold) object. During hypnosis people can engage in automatic writing, spontaneous speech, visual and auditory hallucinations, and alterations in their sense of time and space. They can become less sensitive to pain or more sensitive to memories and perceptions. Within a trance people can envision a new future and begin taking the steps required to actualize that future.

The amazement people experience when presented with such hypnotic phenomena is merely a reflection of their own ignorance regarding the unconscious abilities that we all possess and demonstrate day in and day out without knowing it. There is nothing truly amazing, puzzling, or supernatural about the ability to play and "hear" a vividly imagined or hallucinated air guitar. Some people can do it equally well with or without a hypnotic induction. Similarly, there is nothing unusual about the ability to lose track of the passage of time, to doodle or write without any conscious awareness of the process, or to imagine a different future and to then take steps to accomplish that imagined outcome. Everyone has these abilities, everyone uses them every day in one fashion or another without being aware of it, and everyone can learn how to use them intentionally.

Unfortunately, by the time most people become adults, it is no longer easy for them to use the power of their own imagination to magnify and direct these various abilities. People need a good excuse to allow such unusual things to happen to them and they need help staying calm when they do happen. That is the *raison d'existence* of the hypnotic induction and suggestion process.

Hypnotic inductions are designed to help people enter into a trance (i.e., to pay attention) after which direct or indirect suggestions can be used to tap into the otherwise overlooked and ignored powers of the imagination. Hypnosis does not confer new abilities on anyone. The hypnotic process just offers people a good excuse for allowing such atypical alterations in perception and response to occur, a culturally approved rationalization if you will.

The Nature of a Hypnotic Trance

In order to access or use "hypnotic" abilities, such as the ability to eliminate pain, to hallucinate a particular smell, or to hold a particular position indefinitely, people need to be able to do a few things that most of us find to be quite difficult. They need to be able to pay close attention to one thing for a long time (i.e., go into a trance) and they need to be able to not overreact when something unexpected or unusual happens while they are in that trance. They must pay attention to the desired outcome so that the desired response can happen, and then they have to stay out of the way so that that response can continue to happen, no matter how unusual or even bizarre that response seems. In other words, they have to be able to enter into a trance state, a state of intensely but passively focused attention, and they have to be able to stay there no matter what happens.

Thus, the first step in any hypnotic process is the development of a trance state of mind. This simply means that the person's attention must become exclusively focused, fascinated, or absorbed by one particular thing for an extended period of time. This quiet, passive, and yet intense observation of an internal or external event is, by definition, a trance state. People enter a trance when they listen to music they love, read an engrossing book, watch an entertaining movie, or listen to a wonderful storyteller. They also tend to enter a trance when they play computer games, participate in sports, do something dangerous, or attempt to solve a difficult or challenging puzzle. Any stimulus or activity that generates or requires a highly focused state of concentrated attention can produce a trance. That is why there are driving trances, skiing trances, meditative trances, dancing trances, problem-solving trances, writing trances, movie-watching trances, and reading trances.

Some people enjoy entering into a trance and are good at it, but many people are not very good at it and do not enjoy it. They often say that it feels too much like losing control. These people tend to believe that they are aware of and in charge of what is happening during their ordinary state of conscious awareness and that they become less aware of what is going on and less in control of themselves when they enter into a trance. Nothing could be further from the truth. Our ordinary state of conscious awareness is a state of almost total chaos over which we have very little conscious control. Conscious attention flits from one thing to another so quickly that it is a wonder anything ever gets done.

This is most easily demonstrated by taking a few minutes to just sit and do nothing. Close your eyes, sit in a comfortably erect position, and try to "do nothing" for ten minutes. You will instantly become aware of the impossibility of doing nothing even for several seconds. Unless you are a practiced meditator your mind will keep churning out commentary on every sensation or perception, images will pop up out of nowhere like the pop up ads on a computer, you will feel fidgety and unable to stay still for very long, and soon your eyes will be open and you will be doing something else entirely.

The interior of the conscious mind is like a ten-storey bank of television sets each tuned to a different channel. We are all multitasking all the time, busy keeping track of where we are, what time it is, what we must do next, the effects of what we just did, and the implications of what someone else is doing now. As I have noted previously, we are lucky that we can rely on the unconscious mind to keep us from running into walls because the simple fact is that we are rarely really in charge of what we are saying or doing, rarely really paying attention to what is going on around us, and rarely fully aware of what someone else is saying or doing at any given moment. The paradox is that people who are in a trance state are much more aware of what they are paying attention to and much more in control (albeit via the unconscious parts of the mind) of what they are doing than people who are in an ordinary state of "waking" consciousness.

For example, consider the trances created during NASCAR events or Xbox video games. Driving a car at over 200 miles an hour on a

circular track with 20 other cars going equally fast tends to produce the same kind of single-minded and intensely focused state
of attention that a good hypnotic trance induction generates. So
does trying to complete the top level of a computer game without
using any cheat codes, or scaling a cliff face without a rope. People
in these situations are truly paying attention to what they are
doing and, as a result, are much more competent and free of conscious badgering than are most people most of the time. They also
tend to be much happier in these highly focused trance states,
which is a major reason why they seek out such situations so exuberantly (see Csikszentmihalyi, 1990). Unfortunately, challenging
"trance inducing" events such as these also produce a lot more
physiological activation and stress than we want for our hypnotic
trances. We do want people to be intensely focused, but we want
them to be comfortably relaxed at the same time.

The trances, the states of focused attention that we are looking for,
are more like the state of stunned, open-mouthed, frozen-in-place
captivation that people experience while listening to a fascinating
storyteller or watching an amazing performance of almost any
skill. The astonishing acrobatics of Cirque de Soleil can precipitate
such a trance, as can the artistry of a good magician or musician.
Similarly, the precision, content, and evocative qualities of a masterful painting, sculpture, or poem can capture and transfix attention, just as a great play or a delightful movie can enchant an
audience and, thus, seduce them into an imaginative involvement
in the events of the story.

What sets a hypnotic trance apart from all of these other types of
trance is what the person agrees to pay attention to and do during
that trance. During a hypnotic trance the person agrees, overtly or
by implication, to pay close attention to whatever the hypnotist is
saying and to just let things happen in response to what is being
said without trying to restrain or interfere with them. A hypnotic
subject becomes much more aware of but less "connected" to
internal and external events. Control of sensations, perceptions,
and behaviors is surrendered to the automatic effects of the hypnotist's words on the unconscious part of the mind, just as control
of shifting, throttling, and braking is surrendered to the automatic
reactions of the unconscious mind as it controls the body during a
high speed race. During a hypnotic trance, the internal critic,

censor, or commentator that we call the conscious mind (or Self) relaxes, takes some time off, becomes dissociated from the rest of the mind and body, and just watches whatever is going on in response to the what the hypnotist is saying without judging or interfering in those responses.

Thus, entry into a trance can be described as the loss of a sense of Self. This brings us full circle back to the opening discussion in Chapter 1 about the relationship between losing the sense of Self and the onset of a mystical experience. Getting rid of interference from the conscious critiques and commentary of the conscious Self – entering into a trance – is a necessary precondition for peak performance of any type. As we shall soon see, it also is a necessary, but not sufficient, precondition for the eventual experience of a cosmic transformation in awareness.

Trance is a condition of focused attention. During a trance attention is highly focused and intensely illuminating. During the trance state attention becomes completely absorbed by ongoing perceptions and reactions, time seems to disappear, and responses feel as if they are occurring almost without thinking. A hypnotic "trance" is a state of mind wherein attention is highly focused on what the hypnotist is saying and, for the time being at least, the person is simply observing the responses and reactions that are occurring automatically in response to what the hypnotist is saying. In a hypnotic trance the person has stopped critically evaluating, judging, and censoring any ongoing changes in experience or perception. Events are allowed to happen without comment or concern. The conscious mind is quietly and intently observing whatever is going on with a rather relaxed and peaceful kind of detachment.

Hypnotized subjects are intensely aware of what is happening to them and of what is being said by the hypnotist, but they are aware of these events in a genuinely uncritical way. They are completely absorbed by the hypnotist's message in the same way that the attention of an audience can be completely absorbed by a good story, an outstanding aria, or a remarkable performance of any type. This absorption, this passively observant yet intensely aware state of mind, is a central defining characteristic of a trance of any sort, including a hypnotic trance. The procedure used to help create the passively focused attention of a hypnotic trance is called a trance induction.

The Nature of Trance Induction

The "trance induction" process has been ritually represented in movies and books by spinning spirals, swinging pocket watches, and glaring hypnotists dramatically counting backwards from ten to one while telling subjects over and over again go into a trance. Although such hokey hypnotic trance inductions can actually work for a few people (about 15% of the population), they only work with people who happen to be very good at going into a trance in the first place. These people tend to go into trances on their own. They can easily become lost in a good book or absorbed by the bizarre events of a science fiction movie. They have no trouble suspending their reality orientation and entering into fantasy worlds. They are what researchers in the field call "highly hypnotizable". They are both willing to go into a trance when told to do so and they already know how to do so.

Unfortunately, the traditional directive approaches (such as swinging watches and counting backwards) will not help most people at all because a majority of people are not used to experiencing a trance, much less doing so for several minutes, and they often even have a tendency to "snap out of it" when they finally do start drifting into a trance. They may genuinely want to experience a trance and do their best to cooperate, but either they do not have any idea how to do so or they are uncomfortable doing so. Either way, they need more than being told what to do. They need to have a little help along the way.

Accordingly, each of the scripts presented in this book uses a rather indirect trance induction approach, with a few directives thrown in for good measure. Each script begins with ideas and messages that both gently guide people toward a trance state and help them maintain that trance over time. There are no specific magic words or phrases that will unerringly compel anyone to enter into a trance. What helps one person develop a trance may be completely useless or even annoying for someone else. The idea behind the trance induction processes used at the beginning of each script in this book is to present words and ideas that most people can agree with, words and ideas that are comforting and soothing, words and ideas that help people relax and pay close attention to what is being said to them, words and ideas that are easy to understand and, thus, words and ideas that both allow and encourage people to just sit back and listen. In general, these scripts do not order or direct people to become hypnotized, they invite people to do so and they seduce them into doing so.

The opening trance induction sections of each script demonstrate approaches that are general enough to have a rather broad appeal, but none of them are going to appeal to everyone. One person might be irritated by an induction that uses fishing as an example of a relaxing activity but pleasantly lulled by an induction that includes a discussion of weeding a garden in the early morning. Try different inductions and different induction topics until you find one that is appealing and appropriate given the needs and interests of each individual. The idea is to find something to say that allows each individual to listen to what is being said with the same degree of interest and comfortable absorption shown by a child listening to fairy tales.

It will also help if you talk to the person in a voice tone, speed, and rhythm that is consistent with an intently absorbed trance state of mind. Just as you would not yell at a child while reading a bedtime story or talk so fast that it would be hard to imaginatively follow the story, it is best to keep the pace, tone, and timbre of your voice as slow, low, and regular as possible. Your voice needs to capture and lull attention just as much as the words you are saying do. Once you accept the fact that it is almost impossible for you to talk too slowly, you will be in a much better position to help others experience a trance no matter what you are saying.

As a person develops a trance state of mind, it is as if a door or a window opens inside that allows unconscious patterns of reaction and response to whatever the hypnotist is saying. In a trance state of mind, a clearly described event becomes a clearly imagined event that then seems to become a real event. The boundaries between suggestion, imagination, and reality begin to dissolve. Suggested or described floating becomes imagined floating, and that becomes the internal experience of actually floating.

Suggested numbness becomes imagined numbness, and that becomes the actual experience of numbness.

When the conscious mind stops trying to comment on and be in charge of everything that happens, it then becomes possible for a person to observe their own thoughts, perceptions, and behaviors without concern, no matter how unusual or bizarre they may seem. This, in turn, allows even the most unusual hypnotic responses to continue to develop. Even when an arm begins to move on its own or a hand refuses to let go of an object, a person in a hypnotic trance state can simply observe those events with a detached, dissociated, and perhaps bemused lack of concern.

Facilitating the development of a passively focused trance, therefore, is merely the first step. The next step is figuring out how to use that trance state to facilitate the development of the desired hypnotic reactions and responses. Unfortunately, like hypnotic induction, this rarely is a simple process. Soliciting a response from the unconscious without arousing the suspicions and concerns of the conscious mind can be a tricky business, even when the person is already in a trance. Accordingly, just as there are many different techniques for inducing a trance, there are many different ways to convey a hypnotic suggestion.

The Nature of Hypnotic Suggestions

To produce hypnotic responses, the focused attention of trance must be comfortably and clearly directed toward the desired changes in perception and response. The person must be led to clearly imagine the goal and to stay disconnected from whatever happens next. The idea is to foster a high level of "imaginative involvement" in the desired outcome because a clearly imagined event tends to become a clearly experienced event. If you clearly imagine your hand getting hotter, it will tend to get hotter. If you clearly imagine yourself falling, you will feel like you actually are falling. The comments, ideas, and other forms of communication used to solicit and/or elicit these types of responses are called "hypnotic suggestions".

Like hypnotic inductions, hypnotic suggestions can vary from very direct and authoritarian to very indirect and subtle. On one end of the spectrum, hypnotic suggestions can consist of direct orders to do or experience something while on the other end of the spectrum hypnotic suggestions can be indirect attempts to engage or activate imaginative involvement by the use of implication, poetic metaphors, symbols, and other persuasive techniques. Not surprisingly, direct suggestions are quite simple to construct (for example, "You will now do X, Y or Z.") but they are usually not very effective. Indirect forms of communication and suggestion require considerable forethought and creativity but they also tend to be more universally effective.

Most people do not respond very well to direct orders or to being told what to do, whether they are in a trance or not. Even fewer will just sit back and allow their unconscious minds to obey such commands. Instead, they tend to react negatively and, in some cases, to come out of the trance entirely. Tell me, for example, that my hand is getting heavier and heavier, and the conscious voice in my head will immediately say in a dismissive tone, "No, it is not!", and that hand will not feel heavy. If you want me to experience my hand getting heavier and heavier, you will be much more success-ful if you carefully describe a hand encased in wax or lead or just wonder out loud if my hand has begun to feel heavy yet. Such indirect suggestions are much less likely to create oppositional resistance from me or from anyone else for that matter.

For example, if you want someone to feel warm, perhaps even so warm that they begin sweating, it may be more effective to tell them a story about how hot it was in Phoenix while you were there, and then invite them to vividly remember times when they have been equally hot and sweaty, than it would be to simply order them to begin feeling hot. By alluding to the desired out-comes rather than directly requesting it, the conscious mind is entertained and distracted while the unconscious mind is informed about the goal or purpose of the session and is led to begin producing that outcome. The more imaginatively immersed the conscious mind is in what the hypnotist is saying, the more distracted it is and the easier it will be for the unconscious mind to generate responses to the images and/or events being described by the hypnotist. The desired hypnotic responses then seem to occur automatically, often without a conscious awareness that anything unusual has occurred at all.

The scripts in this book use metaphorical implications, anecdotes, similes, puns, poetic wordings, and a poetic structure, some of which are included to help create and maintain the focused attention of the trance state of mind and some of which are designed to convey indirect suggestions. Metaphorical and symbolic references are used to capture and redirect attention in a way that indirectly implies and promotes the desired outcome. The stories, word games, rhymes, and rhythms contained in these scripts are puzzling, engaging, and even quite confusing at times, which can add to the depth of the trance and can also allow for a more profound and uncensored response than might otherwise be feasible. By keeping the attention of the conscious mind engaged elsewhere with confusing and/or entrancing wordings, rhymes, rhythms, and puns, the hypnotist makes it possible for the unconscious mind to respond more freely and completely to the underlying implications of the overall narrative.

For example, telling someone to "wait patiently for the weight of the world to be lifted a foot or more from the heaviest foot on one leg or the other" is a confusing and playful way to distract the conscious mind while also suggesting (via implication) an experience of heaviness in one foot or the other. By contrast, telling someone authoritatively that their left foot will become too heavy to lift when you count to five, and then counting to five in a dramatic tone of voice, rarely has the intended effect. Mentioning the desired outcome in passing, alluding to it in a confusing way, describing an example of it, or just inviting the person to wonder how it would feel if that outcome occurred are much more effective techniques for engaging the imagination and luring the person into experiencing the desired outcome because they do not challenge the conscious mind to a duel over control.

The basic rule is to use verbal stratagems that help people experience the desired effect rather than just trying to force them to obey instructions or to do things that they do not know how to do. And because it is impossible ahead of time to predict exactly which approach will be the most helpful for any given individual, the scripts presented in the next section of this book all use a variety of techniques pointed toward the same outcome in the hope that at least one of them will succeed in stimulating that response.

To summarize, each hypnotic script presented in the following chapters begins with soothing and attention-compelling comments designed to serve as a trance induction. This trance induction process is then followed by one or more references to concepts, images, and events that provide indirect or implied suggestions for the desired responses. These analogical, metaphorical, and symbolic references are presented in a poetic format designed to capture attention, distract or calm the conscious mind, and indirectly or associatively solicit the desired response. In addition, one or more direct suggestions for the desired response are often embedded within the presentation. Thus, each script contains many different opportunities for the desired response to develop and each is permissive and gentle enough to avoid any implication of failure or inadequacy. No matter what happens or what the person experiences, the goal is to leave each participant with the understanding that what they experienced was perfectly normal, appropriate, and ultimately useful.

The Nature of Trance Termination

Eventually every hypnotic session must come to an end. Even if the hypnotist just got up and walked out in the middle of a session, everyone would eventually wake up from or terminate the trance state. No one gets stuck in a trance. Left to their own devices, people in a trance will either open their eyes and reorient themselves within a short time or simply drift off into sleep and wake up from their nap a bit later.

Nonetheless, it is traditional and appropriate for the person ostensibly in charge, the hypnotist, to tell the participant when it is time to begin waking up, coming out of the trance, and becoming more aware of the immediate environment. Like everything else about the hypnotic procedures used in this text, this "trance termination" process is handled in a rather gentle and gradual fashion. A slow reorientation makes it a pleasant and effortless drifting back into ordinary conscious awareness rather than a sudden or forced jolt back to reality.

Just as there is no absolutely right thing to say during a trance induction process, there is no absolutely right thing to say during a trance termination process. Many different statements can be used to guide attention and awareness gently back toward the surface of consciousness. The scripts in this book each end in a slightly different fashion with somewhat different trance termination directions, depending on what came before, but all are very similar in many respects as well.

One thing many of the scripts have in common is that they include a direct or indirect suggestion for positive effects down the road, long after that particular trance session has ended. In some cases there is even an indication that an intense enlightenment experience might occur suddenly and unexpectedly at some later date. Setting up an optimistic anticipation of a peak or transcendent experience enhances the likelihood that such an experience will, in fact, occur. It can easily become a self-fulfilling prophecy. Looking around expectantly for such an experience is a delightful way to pass the time in any case and it is something I would recommend to everyone, whether or not a hypnotic trance is involved.

Some hypnotherapists include suggestions during the trance termination process for subjects to forget much, if not all, of what happened throughout the preceding session. This use of post-hypnotic amnesia in a therapeutic setting is designed to protect the knowledge gained during the session from conscious distortions and misinterpretations. Post-hypnotic amnesia also is frequently used by stage hypnotists, although they use it to demonstrate the supposed "power" of hypnosis rather than for any ostensible benefits for the participants. Because post-hypnotic amnesia is now such a widely recognized aspect of hypnosis, it often occurs spontaneously just because the general public has been led to expect it. But if a session is going to have longstanding consequences, then the events of that session cannot be allowed to be repressed or eradicated from memory entirely.

Accordingly, the trance termination instructions presented at the end of each script in this book usually include the idea that some things can be left behind until later and others may not belong in awareness at all, but that some things can be remembered quite easily and brought back fully into wakeful awareness. Although memories of the session may fade somewhat as a natural result of state specific learning and some parts of the session may never be recovered, specifically instructing subjects to remember useful aspects of the experience helps insure that some things will remain in memory afterwards.

Hypnotic experiences naturally tend to have a dreamlike quality to them as well. Some things will be remembered vaguely, others uncertainly, and only a few quite clearly. But the impact or aftereffects of a hypnotic session can continue having reverberating effects even though the person does not remember much about it at all. And it is also important to remember that some aspects of a hypnotic session may not be remembered or appreciated until long after the person has returned to ordinary wakeful awareness. We can give people opportunities and invitations to remember but what each individual remembers is ultimately dependent on the needs and interest of that particular individual.

The same could be said for how and when a person finally emerges from the trance state. No matter how directive or non-directive the suggestions are for returning to wakeful awareness and opening the eyes, some people will resist the process and take a long time to reorient and some people will snap right out of it. Once you have conveyed the notion that it is time for the session to come to an end, which is usually pretty obvious right away, the rest of what you say is mostly a matter of reassuring and facilitating that reorientation process and giving the person time to adjust to the idea. Abrupt arousals from sleep, reverie or hypnotic trances are just not very pleasant.

If a participant prefers to stay in the trance state after the script has ended – oh well! Unless I happen to be in a hurry, my usual response to such a situation is to tell the person that they can reorient whenever they are ready and then sit back and wait patiently. Sometimes this even turns out to be the most productive part of the hypnosis session.

Eventually, after allowing for a suitable period of readjustment or reorientation, it is appropriate to simply tell people to open their eyes and wake up. Most will do so immediately, some after a few more reluctant seconds, and, rarely, only after several more minutes and even more direct instructions to do so. On the other hand, if the person is just asleep, which you can be sure of if you hear snoring, then gently wake them up the way you would anyone who falls asleep while you are talking to them.

Developing a Self-Hypnotic Approach

A majority of people find it easier to experience hypnotic events when those events are directed by another person. Once they have gone through a hypnotic session directed by someone else then they can re-create that experience simply by contemplating the memory of it. A clearly remembered trance becomes a trance.

Thus, not all hypnotic trances require a hypnotist. A self-directed self-hypnotic approach can be quite effective and any of the scripts presented in this text can be used as the basis for a self-hypnotic session. Although I do believe that self hypnosis is much easier to master if you have first gone through at least one session conducted by a competent hypnotist, I also am firmly convinced that anyone can become their own best hypnotist. All it takes is an open mind, an optimistic anticipation of success, and a clear idea of the goal or purpose of the session. (Of course, an open mind, a positive attitude, and a commitment to a specific outcome are helpful for all hypnotic endeavors, whether they involve self-hypnosis or hetero-hypnosis).

Once you learn how to use self hypnosis to enter a trance and to experience specific alterations in sensation or response, you can either direct that trance toward specific hypnotic events, such as those described in the scripts presented in this book, or you can use it for personal growth, comfortable self awareness, problem solving, enhanced creativity, pain management, or basic relaxation. If nothing else, you can always use it to just sit back and give your unconscious mind an opportunity to take you wherever it thinks would be a useful and healing place to go.

Because self hypnosis can be an incredibly valuable tool, here are some quick and easy tests of your self-hypnotic potential. Use the exercises below to determine just how responsive you are to your own imaginatively generated hypnotic suggestions.

1. Hold an arm out in front of you, straight out. Now, close your eyes and imagine a weight pushing down on it or pulling down on it. Imagine that weight as clearly as you can. Imagine that you are holding a dumbbell or a bucket or water. If your arm starts to move down within 15 or 20 seconds, then you have promising self-hypnotic abilities.
2. Sit in a relaxed position, close your eyes and imagine yourself suddenly falling backwards, as if the ground has just opened up and you are falling backwards into a vast chasm. If you feel a stomach churning sense of vertigo as you do so or find it difficult to not open your eyes and "snap out of it", then your self-hypnotic capacities are excellent.
3. Imagine sucking on a slice of lemon. If your salivary glands react to that imagined sourness, then you have the ability to hypnotically alter your experience quite effectively.
4. Another way to assess your hypnotic capacities is to ask yourself if you tend to get lost in a good book or movie. Do you get lost playing video games? Do you become so absorbed in any or all tasks that you lose track of time?

If all four of the above describe you, then you may have a very high degree of hypnotic responsiveness. If you can become so absorbed in an activity that you get lost in it or if you can imagine an experience so vividly that it seems real, real enough to provoke an actual physical or emotional response, then you may be so responsive that you can use a direct hypnotic suggestions with yourself to imagine and stimulate whatever kinds of perceptual or cognitive changes you wish, including those changes commonly associated with a cosmic state of mind. If that is the case, then all you have to do is decide which of the phenomena to start with, sit back, close your eyes, relax, and begin imagining that intense white light, overwhelmingly beautiful sound or whatever aspect of the mystical experience seems the most appealing to you.

Most people will find that it is not quite this easy. If you are like a majority of the population then you can focus your attention and imagine things reasonably well, but you will still need some help allowing yourself to experience the kinds of changes in perception and cognition that we are dealing with here. Ordinarily this would be the role of the hypnotist, but if you are going to do this yourself, then you need to find a way to serve as both the hypnotist who is guiding and directing things and, simultaneously, as the subject who is quietly observing and going along with the process. This is only a bit more difficult than letting someone else serve as the hypnotist and there are several options for how to accomplish it.

One way that you can serve as your own hypnotist is by memorizing the basic outline and contents of a script and then silently repeating those ideas to yourself. First, find and read through a script that appeals to you until you feel like you know it reasonably well. You do not have to memorize it in detail, just familiarize yourself with the central points. Then sit quietly in a place where you will not be disturbed, close your eyes, and relax. Once you begin to feel relaxed then start reviewing the words or ideas that you remember from that script. Focus your attention on those ideas and allow your mind to drift along into the experiences described by it. You can either "talk" to yourself in your own thoughts or you can imagine someone else saying those things to you. Try doing it each way and see which one works best for you. On the other hand, you may prefer to make a recording of a script so that you do not have to play both roles at the same time. You can then relax and listen to a recording just as you would if you were listening to a hypnotist talking to you.

Whether you intend to record a script or repeat it to yourself in your mind, you do not have to use any of the scripts in this book. They are merely instructive examples. If you have read the preceding chapters then you already know exactly what you are trying to accomplish and what is involved in that effort. It also is likely that you already have some idea of how you would like to try to accomplish that goal. You probably already have a sense of what elements of the mystical state are most appealing or comfortable to contemplate and you probably already have some thoughts about what someone else would have to say to help you experience those things. Accordingly, it is very likely that a script designed for you by you would be more useful than anything I could create.

Creating your own hypnosis script is similar to mixing a CD of dance music to suit your own specific tastes. You can begin by finding examples of things that capture your attention, whether from the hypnosis scripts presented in this or other books or from poems, scriptures, CDs, or just words and phrases that fascinate you. The parts that capture your attention are the parts that you mix together for the induction phase of a trance. The parts that stimulate your imagination in a way that moves it toward visual, auditory, or sensory experiences typical of cosmic consciousness are the parts that you will want to emphasize after that.

As you read through each of the scripts in this book, therefore, make a note of any induction or suggestion procedures that are particularly appealing to you or of any parts of a script that seem especially interesting and involving. It is fine to mix and match the different types of induction and suggestion procedures used in these scripts to create an approach that feels right or makes sense to you. Because all hypnosis actually is self hypnosis, you are the only legitimate expert when it comes to your own willingness and ability to respond to a particular idea or suggestion. If something is comfortable and captivating, then it is worth incorporating into your own personal script.

Once you have selected the various captivation (induction), imagination (suggestion) and reorientation (awakening) procedures that you want to use, write them all out in a way that describes the journey you want to take. Begin with changes in sensation or awareness that are comfortable and involve relatively small alterations of your ordinary state of mind. Then add ideas or concepts that seem a bit more unusual or challenging. The purpose is to move gradually but inexorably toward the desired outcome in a way that allows you to stay relaxed and comfortable even as you begin experiencing things that ordinarily might be difficult to imagine or tolerate. Every now and then as you are creating this session for yourself, just stop, close your eyes, and imagine listening to someone saying those same things to you. As long as it feels comfortable and enticing, keep it in the script. If it begins to sound awkward or confusing, back up a few steps and try a different suggestion or image instead. Ideally, the end product should feel as smooth as silk when you listen to it, as warm and soothing as a massage, and as engaging as the best movie you have ever seen.

If you do record a hypnosis session to use yourself, either one that you have constructed for yourself or one that you have selected from those provided in this book, you may find that you tend to drift into a trance as you read it out loud. This is a good indication that the script you are using is right for you. If it is compelling and involving even when you are actively trying to stay detached from it, then it is almost guaranteed to be effective when you surrender to it.

You may, of course, have someone else read a script to you or have them make a recording of it for you. That is fine. No matter how you decide to present a hypnotic session to yourself, just close your eyes, listen to the words, and drift away with your own ideas of where you want to go and how you want to get there.

I mentioned above that all hypnosis is self hypnosis. There is nothing startling or new in this statement. If you stop and think about it for even a moment, it should be obvious that this is the case. Hypnosis is not something that is done *to* you; hypnosis is something that is done *by* you. As a professional hypnotherapist, all I can do is say things in ways that I think will entice and enable others to begin using their own hypnotic abilities. Whether they do so or not is entirely up to them. I cannot force anyone to enter into a trance or do my bidding. Again, there are no supernatural powers, magical incantations, or voice inflections that give hypnotists access to or control over the thoughts, behaviors, or experiences of anyone else. Each hypnotic subject is responsible for what happens, all of the events are generated by that person. If you are going to experience a trance, you will have to allow yourself to become entranced. If you are going to respond to various suggestions for altered sensations and perceptions, you will have to allow those things to happen to you. It all belongs to you and the only way to determine the best way for you to direct your own hypnosis session is to try several different techniques. Experience is the best teacher.

Some people find it very easy to do these things. The brief tests of your ability to imagine that were presented above offer a quick estimate of your current hypnotic responsiveness. If each of them applies to you, or if any one of them has a very powerful impact, then, as I said before, it is likely that you have a relatively high capacity for hypnotic involvement. In fact, you probably use your hypnotic capacity for imaginative involvement all the time without even realizing it. This is important to note because even a briefly imagined event can have a profound effect on people with a high hypnotic responsiveness. Such briefly imagined events can be affirming, enhancing, and pleasurable, but they also can be frightening or disturbing. An imagined plane crash can quickly lead to a problematic fear of flying. An imagined attack can produce very real panic. If you are a person who has a high degree of hypnotic responsiveness, therefore, it is very important for you to learn how to use it for your own benefit and how to avoid using it to your own detriment. Unfortunately, helping you learn this is not the purpose of the present book. Becoming familiar with and mastering the full range of hypnotic responses is an involved and complex process. Therefore, if after trying the brief hypnotizability test above you have reason to believe that you are highly hypnotizable, I urge you to consult a trained hypnotherapist to learn more about directing all of your hypnotic responses in positive directions.

In the meantime, for those of you who are not highly responsive to imagined events, rest assured that persistence and practice in the pursuit of your own self-managed hypnotic experience will eventually pay off. The same could be said for anyone working with a professional hypnotist. Even if it feels awkward or unproductive at first, stick with it and eventually you will feel a finger move automatically, one hand become significantly hotter or colder than the other, or a bright light off in the distance move closer and closer and get brighter and brighter until it takes over your entire existence. When that begins to happen, just relax and enjoy the fireworks.

Entering into a transcendent experience and allowing cosmic consciousness to overtake you is a bit like riding a roller coaster with your arms up and a smile on your face. You must surrender to the inevitable and decide to endure the seemingly unendurable. You must trust that it is safe to keep going even when it feels like everything is about to fall apart and fly off in all directions. You must trust your unconscious mind to take care of you no matter where it takes you or what things it suddenly begins to show you. So relax, stop holding on, and just let things happen even when it feels like the earth is falling out from under you.

Section II

Scripts

Be advised that the scripts presented in the following chapters are designed to be listened to in a relaxed and accepting state of mind, a state of mind that allows the words to reverberate through awareness, redirect attention in particular ways, and evoke various conscious and unconscious reactions. They are not designed to be read in an ordinary wakeful state of mind in an effort to critically decipher their meaning. Reading them to yourself the way you would a book or a magazine article will not produce much, if any, effect other than puzzlement and/or confusion. To experience their intended meanings and implications you have to listen to them quietly without trying to figure them out, the same way you would listen to a piece of music or a poem.

Please also be advised that these scripts are printed in a format designed to convey the proper rhythm of presentation: brief phrases presented slowly, several words at a time, with pauses in between to give people a chance to "ponder" the words and to experience the associations and reactions created by those words. It is almost impossible to speak too slowly to someone in a trance. Force yourself to read these scripts as slowly as you can and you will be speaking slowly enough for others to really hear what is being said and to respond to it.

Chapter 6

Hypnotic Immersions in Light

Vision is clearly the most dominant and useful source of information about the real world for most people. We all rely heavily on visual input to show us where we are and what is going on, to clarify the meaning of sounds and sensations, and to monitor the behavior of others. We even organize our thoughts and memories around visual representations of things real and imagined. What we see is what we believe.

It is not surprising, therefore, that light is a core element of almost all religious, spiritual, and transcendental experiences. Light is often associated with the arrival of a god or other supernatural being. Light, in the form of a halo or aura, is used as a visual manifestation of our human essence or soul and as a representation of inner purity. And a sudden eruption of an intense, unbearably brilliant white light or fire, a light that no one else can see but that seems to penetrate everything, is often a central component of religious conversions and other transformational rearrangements of thought or awareness.

Obviously, it is no coincidence that the terms "illumination", "enlightenment", "brilliance", "brightness", "luminescence", and "radiance" all refer both to light and to the human mind or spirit. We are seekers of illumination, blinding flashes of it and enduring immersions in it. No one wants to be left out in the dark. We all want to see truth in a sudden explosion of enlightenment.

Thus, even though it sounds like a tautology, it can be said that illumination produces illumination. That, in any event, is the assumption underlying this chapter. The scripts presented here are designed to lead the mind toward an awareness of an illumination, an awareness of brilliance within the mind's eye that eventually expands to encompass all understanding and all experience.

91

If nothing else, such ideas sow seeds that may burst forth in a dream or a daydream months or years later. And even an imagined brilliance can light up many dark corners in the back of the mind.

A Distant Star

Now,
you can just sit there
in that chair
with your eyes closed
becoming aware
that you can become
even more relaxed over time,
even more comfortable
in this short time
than you were before,
are you not,
but not yet as much
as you will be later on,
because you can take your time
to drift into a trance,
a state of quiet awareness,
a quiet recognition
of all those things
that I could say
as you sit here today,
waiting for me to say something
that will change your experience,
that will alter your life
forever,
but also being afraid,
being worried that I will say
just the right thing
to change things for you,
to alter your life
forever,
but remember that all change
actually belongs just to you,
and only you can change things for you,
change things within you, because all I can do

is talk about things
while you can allow those things,
and many other things,
to come true for you,
to happen within you,
the same way a dream
can seem to be true for you,
and in your mind's eye
you can see things
in that dream
that are very close or very far away,
even with your eyes closed,
the way you can now,
things as far away
as a star,
a tiny star,
a bright point of light
way up there at night
in the mind's eye,
so very far away
that you can only wonder
what would it be like
to travel to that star,
as if in a dream,
moving toward that tiny light
faster and faster,
faster than light,
flying through the night
looking out at it,
seeing that star getting closer and closer,
growing larger and larger,
becoming brighter and brighter
and eventually filling up the sky,
becoming so bright,
not just a star any more,
becoming a sun,
an enormous sun,
much bigger than our sun,
and you know how bright
sunlight can be,
the way walking out of a dark theater

into the light of day
can almost be painful,
too bright to keep your eyes open,
and this sun is even brighter than that perhaps
and getting even brighter now,
because it is not just one sun,
not like our sun,
but a galaxy of suns,
a thousand points of brilliant light,
a million billion points of brilliant light,
all around you everywhere,
illuminating everything, everywhere,
surrounding everything, everywhere
and as you move closer to the center,
the center of all those stars,
all that starlight sunlight
shining into you,
coming into and through you,
right into your mind,
those bright lights behind you
and that intense light above you
and that white light below you,
starlight on all sides of you
and a light deep within you,
a sun in the center of your mind
that goes on and on,
bigger and bigger,
as you go on and on
feeling that inner light,
that center starlight there,
becoming that light everywhere,
that sun at the center of it all,
feeling that energy
of all that light
passing right on through you,
flowing out from you,
as you become that light,
that lightness of being light
and of making light of things,
and discovering over time
that you can make light out of anything

and make anything out of light,
including all those thoughts
that you hear and feel and see,
and wondering how it sounds,
all that energy of light within you
and all that light roaring out from you,
like the roar of a blast furnace
behind that door of the mind
where a white hot roar
of sound surrounds
and becomes the sound of light,
a light you can feel now
in your arms and hands,
legs and feet,
an intense white heat
of that light that roars
right through you,
and bursts out from you
and sizzles within you
all at the same time,
all around you now,
all around the mind
like a star being born,
a star forming in space,
a universe of stars,
performing in space,
a space within you
a universe within you
lit up with stars
that give light to you,
a child of the sun,
becoming a sun,
and discovering how it feels
to dissolve into light,
arms nothing but light,
legs nothing but light,
the mind nothing but light
moving from one place to another
scattering colors all around,
lighting up every corner of awareness
and then gradually collapsing

coming together now
into a beam of light
like a laser beam,
a bright spotlight that shines
straight out from the mind
straight up into the sky
announcing something special
and illuminating everything it touches,
creating everything you notice,
with a recognition
that the only things that do exist
are the things you allow into your mind
and now is a very good time
to open up the mind
to all those things
that otherwise
would tend to go overlooked
or ignored,
allowing the light of the mind to expand
and to include everything out there,
to touch everything out there,
to allow the universe into you
and to allow that light within you
to shine warmly on it all,
so you can feel it all
as a part of you,
all connected to you,
reflected right back at you
like the light in a mirror
that lets you see yourself
so much more clearly
than before,
and lets you see now
that all there is is you
sitting there
doing it all,
creating it all,
or is it being created for you?
I can tell you about a man
who traveled all the way to Arizona
just to watch some videos

of a famous hypnotist
working with different people,
talking to them about being in a trance,
wondering about their memories,
asking about their experiences,
telling them about unlimited possibilities
and letting them learn
in their own way,
what he had learned
in his own way,
and that man sat there
in that room all day
watching those videos,
taking careful notes about everything said,
then he flew home,
put his notes away,
and continued to see his own clients,
continued doing hypnotherapy,
continued teaching at the university,
and began writing books and giving lectures,
got invited to do workshops,
wrote more books
and gave more lectures,
and one day twenty years later
he found those notes again,
and as he read through them
he began smiling
because on each page
were words and ideas
that he thought he had invented
when he wrote his books
and gave his lectures,
but actually were implanted
deep in his understandings
by watching what that other man said
so many years before
that he had forgotten all about,
or so he thought before,
but here was evidence
that we never really know
where what we do or say,

or even what we think,
really came from in the first place,
because we can forget the source
but our understandings are still there,
and so we can be sure
that when we hear something we can use
we will absorb it,
and make it our own,
and put it to good use,
without knowing or needing to know
where we got it or when,
because the truth is
that all you need to do
to find illumination
is to pay close attention
to what you already know
and what you already have experienced,
it all belongs to you,
which is why later on
today or tomorrow or next week,
you can begin to notice
that you can bring that feeling,
the idea of that feeling,
your understanding of it all
back into you
where it can light up
those inner spaces
in ways you have yet to see,
while in the meantime here today
you begin to see
that you really are here right now,
and you can be here now
while you remember
being there then
and drift back into this place now
away from the star light there then,
away from the star dust,
and back with the memories,
the star dust memories,
being here and now
close to where you began

but someplace different now,
a different time and space,
a different place inside,
with something inside changed,
something easier
and more comfortable,
something quieter
and more powerful,
something stronger
and more understanding,
forged in the fires of the mind,
in white hot steel and blazing fire
that forms a solid core
that is a part of it all,
of all that energy
in everything out there,
all that energy within you
even as you continue
to wonder what it is
that you have learned from you today
because first you know the answer,
and then it slips away,
so you look for another answer
and it slips away too,
and then it all breaks through
into your awareness,
a glimpse of understanding
that hovers there with you
as you begin drifting up now
more and more completely
and gradually return
back into wakeful awareness
now,
that's right,
drifting back
to the sound of my voice,
to being here in this room,
to being aware of arms and legs,
but holding on
to where you have been
and to where you ended up,

in that solid brilliant core
in the center of you,
connected to it all,
comfortable with it all,
knowing something
you did not know you knew before
but comfortable understanding
that you do not need to know
what that knowledge is right now
or what it holds in store
for later on,
as you drift up into wakeful awareness,
gradually reaching a point
of wakefulness now
where the eyes
can begin to feel
like opening,
that's right,
your eyes opening comfortably
now
and the mind returning
quite completely now
to wakeful awareness,
wide awake again,
comfortably awake
now,
that's right,
wide awake.

Be Your Own Light
Now, while you sit there
and continue to relax,
staring at a particular spot
on the back of your hand
and noticing that feeling
of letting the mind relax
so that you can drift down
into a deeply comfortable
state of mind
where you can listen comfortably,
without having to try to make an effort

100

to do anything at all,
I can be reminded of a time
many years ago
as a student
when I first walked past an office door
that was covered with comics and pictures,
short articles and long essays,
bumper stickers and postcards
that a professor had taped up there,
posting small pieces of thought
for all to think about briefly
and to consider adding
to their own collections
of understandings and memories,
but one of them stood out,
jumped out at passersby,
shouting out at them
in bold purple letters,
"Be your own light!", it said,
"Do not depend on others!",
as if to emphasize
that all of these postings
were the insights of others,
and might not light the way
toward one's own illumination,
which instantly raised the question
of where to find that light
to light your own way
and how to use that light
to light the way
along those paths
to some unknown end
that actually is a beginning,
and how to avoid
getting lost along the way,
how to become your own light,
perhaps like the very bright light
of a special spotlight
that comes with its own warning
to not look at it directly
or touch the bulb while it is lit

because it is so hot and bright,
a light that can send a beam of light
across a two-mile wide lake
and light up houses on the opposite shore,
which is a very bright light indeed,
but if you cannot look at it
without injuring yourself
how safe can it be
and how useful for reading
the wisdom of the ages
while sitting in a comfortable chair there,
so you might want to consider
finding something softer
if you are going to be your own light
while not depending on others
to find your way,
you might want to use
something gently illuminating,
like a candle perhaps,
which at first might seem quite dim
and not adequate at all,
until you imagine one inside your mind
and remember staring at that flame
in the quiet darkness,
a small candle flame,
a yellow flickering light
that we sometimes use to see by
when the electricity goes out,
a light that seemed very dim at first,
compared to a bright light bulb,
but gets brighter over time
as we adjust to it,
soon lights up an entire room,
fills up all the corners
of every space inside,
the way that light inside you,
that light that you become
when you use your imagination
can fill your mind as well,
and illuminate
every corner

just enough to see
just enough to explore
all the hidden understandings
and the long forgotten truths
stored away deep down inside,
away from the light of day,
because a candle in the mind
does not light up things
with a sudden blinding brilliance
like a match in a pitch black room,
an instant blaze of light
with a sizzle of sound,
that makes us turn away at first
until it settles down,
and we can see again
to use that match
to light a candle or a flare,
a soft light or a bright one,
they both light up the night,
the dark spaces in the mind,
while you drift into the center
and find that one light
that belongs to you,
because a becoming light
that makes you look good
is different from becoming a light,
that makes you feel good
and seeing that light
in the back of the mind
that at first may seem very far away,
is just the first step
to feeling that light
getting closer and closer,
becoming larger and larger,
so close you can touch it,
feel the heat of it,
the energy of it
lighting up your skin,
lighting up your muscles,
lighting up everything inside,
and lighting up this room as well,

filling all those spaces out here,
a light so large you can hear it,
can hear the orchestral roar of it,
with a sound so loud
that it vibrates everything
and you can feel it,
that most beautiful sound of all
vibrating in your chest,
the way you can feel speakers vibrate
with a deep rumbling roar,
vibrating every fiber of you,
a heavenly choir,
a heavenly roar
sending that sound
right through you
and out into everything
until that light becomes so bright,
so unbearably beautifully bright,
and the sound becomes so intense,
so intensely emotionally amazing,
that the mind may keep trying
to turn away from it all
and find it difficult to stay right there
where it has been hard to be before,
a familiar place you have been to before,
but a scary place
to just fall into,
a place where you are free to be,
a place to be your own light,
a place to be light,
a place to feel light,
lighter than air at times,
freer than light at times,
free to light up the sky at times,
and free now to take your own time
to become lighter than light,
brighter than bright,
and just be a flame
that lights up your mind
and shows you things
that might otherwise go overlooked,

how things can seem to be one thing
and turn out to be something else entirely,
the way two and two can be four,
but before you know it,
two can become three
because baby makes three,
and you were young once,
a mere babe in the woods,
before it all
separated out
into different things,
and someone invented ideas
about inside and out,
or up and down,
or good and bad,
each defined by the other,
each existing
only because of the other,
neither one really there at all,
not really anywhere at all,
nowhere is there an up or a down
except our thinking makes it so,
and so as you explore your thinking
and light your own path
your mind can discover
how it feels to light up
all those things that you usually ignore,
and find out how it feels
to explore those things
that we all take for granted
without stopping to wonder
where all of this stuff came from
and what would it be like
to just clean the mind out,
to empty it all out
and start over from scratch,
a blank slate,
no ideas but your own,
no myths to ignore,
no superstitions to disprove,
no fantasies to escape,

no ignorance to overlook,
no words for anything,
nothing to believe unless you make it so,
and so you can just know whatever you know
and let go of all the rest,
and try being your own light,
lighting your own way,
finding the truth for you
right now,
that's right,
take your time,
let things settle out
the way water clears
when you just let it sit
and then the light
can shine through it,
can get through it to out you,
even as you begin to remember
places you have walked
and seen things posted
on office doors,
things to think about,
ideas to consider,
quotations from famous people,
notations about the speed of light,
and jokes at their own expense,
things to consider
while the mind drifts back and forth now
for a while,
back to this room,
and then back wondering
where it has been
and what it learned from itself,
and then back again here now
toward the surface of wakefulness,
more and more fully awake and alert,
and then back down again a little bit,
wondering what it all means,
and back upwards again,
knowing exactly what it means
on the one hand,

with no idea what it means on the other,
even as you continue to drift upwards,
feeling rested and refreshed,
some things remaining behind,
others remembered clearly
in the light of day,
like notes posted on office doors,
easily seen and easily understood,
as you drift up more completely now,
upwards enough to allow your eyes to open
as wakeful awareness returns
quite completely now,
that's right,
the light fades
into the background
as the mind drifts
into the foreground
and you return
and become wide awake now,
eyes open and
the mind awake
quite completely.

Brilliant Ideas

Just relax there for a moment
and start going into a trance
while I take some time
to consider the things I am going to say,
but don't drift down too quickly,
take some time to let that trance develop,
to let it grow and become comfortable for you
because a trance is just a state
of being comfortable
while you pay close attention to things
that otherwise you might overlook,
while at the same time
you do not need to pay much attention at all
to things that ordinarily you would,
like the things I might say
and whether or not they make sense to you,
which is not something

you need to pay much attention to
or be concerned about
because you have an unconscious mind
and it can take care of those things for you,
it can continue to hear the things I say
even while your conscious mind drifts away
someplace else entirely,
off to a warm soft beach
or a snow covered mountain
or any place that appeals to you,
where your mind
can just ride along
with the sound of my voice
wherever the words might take you
without trying to figure out
just where that might be
or what you might see
along the way,
which is not something
that I am ready to talk about
quite yet,
so you can just continue
to try to figure out
how to enter into a trance
on your own
and I will continue
to try to figure out
what to say to you
to help you do so
in the most comfortable way possible,
but also what to say to you
to allow you to experience
a lovely transformation
in your own imagination
about your own experience
that leads to an awareness
of something long overlooked
that you are seeking here today,
perhaps that tiny, tiny point of light
in the back of the mind,
down in the center of awareness,

so tiny it is out of sight
most of the time
and completely out of mind
the rest of the time,
but so intensely bright that it is difficult
to not look at it,
and hard to look at
without blinking,
which makes it doubly difficult
to locate it exactly,
something too teeny tiny to see
and too incredibly bright to look at,
a difficult thing to locate,
even in the imagination,
but it is really there
and you can find it
when you relax just a little more
and stop worrying about it,
or even thinking about it,
and just drift into that trance
that you are drifting into now
and just continue to allow yourself
to let go,
to let go of all the effort it takes
to not drift in that direction,
to not make that connection,
because each time you let go
the mind drifts that way
automatically,
attracted to that light
like a moth to a flame,
and all you need to do
is nothing at all
and you will drift
right down into it
effortlessly,
right into the center of it
automatically,
doing nothing
but allowing it to occur,
remaining relaxed and comfortable

even though you keep getting closer
and the bright intensity keeps growing,
and that tiny intensity of sensation and feeling,
of sound and fury
signifying nothing
and everything at the same time
begins feeling like everything
all at the same time,
intense sensations and intense emotions,
intense brilliance and unbearable heat,
with a sound that reverberates through the bones
and a light so bright
that you cannot look at it
but cannot turn away from it either,
intensities of light and sound that grow
as the mind is pulled into them,
and each time you relax
even a little bit,
you can drift more in that direction,
pulled in that direction
as if by a magnet
that gets stronger and stronger
like an irresistible force
from such a tiny but powerful place,
which is why we try
to ignore it or to pretend
that it does not exist,
even though you have been there before,
in childhood perhaps,
and that is why it is so easy to find
by not doing anything at all,
just quieting the mind
into the calm smoothness
of a still pond
without even a ripple
except deep inside
going into that tiny bright spot
that turns out to be
a massive doorway,
an open passage into a brilliant space,
a connecting point to another place,

a path into another way of being,
a connection of each to all,
a place where we all begin and end,
a drop of energy that marks the start
of doors that open into a space,
a place where we were before
we were born
and where we go later on,
a fiery force of energy
hidden away deep down inside,
so far away it stays away,
forgotten and hidden,
until you relax
and allow the mind to drift that way,
drawn into it automatically,
returning to it automatically,
and each time you go that way
it gets easier and easier to do it,
easier and easier to endure it,
to allow it to get brighter and brighter,
more and more intense in every way,
unbearably overwhelming,
until it sweeps the mind away
and becomes all there is
inside and out,
replaces thought and sensation,
takes over sight and sound,
intensifies it all,
and then creates emotions
too powerful to control,
like riding a wave
of constant connection
to everything everywhere,
all sights and sounds,
all thoughts and feelings,
all of everything all at once,
that you can continue to explore
while I consider what more to say
to help you stay,
not falling away too quickly
into a deep and comfortable trance

where it might become difficult
to not be unaware of that point of light
that keeps drawing you in
until you are already there,
surrounded by it,
immersed within it,
better to take it step by step,
to drift toward it one step at a time,
to feel and see it getting closer and closer,
to allow the mind time to adjust
to the ever increasing brightness,
the way we adjust to sparklers
in the darkness on the Fourth of July,
sparklers that flare with the brightness
of a flashbulb going off at night
that never stops staying on,
that never stops being too bright
to look at directly,
but you really do not need
to make the effort it might take
to move into that light completely
and to let that light pass right through you
so you could come out on the other side,
like falling down and through
a brilliant and deep well
that gets more intense
the deeper you go,
down where that chorus of sound
from all that light
can be felt as well as heard,
down where the vibrations
of light and sound
rebound right through you
and move out into
everything around you
in a way that allows you
to feel it all,
to touch it all,
to become a part of it all,
to feel your mind
move out through the walls,

out into the air
out into the minds of others,
out into the stars,
and out to the ends of the universe
and on and on,
where it may seem like
no one has gone before
but you can also know
that you do not have to go anywhere,
and that everyone else can get there,
because we are all already there,
somewhere deep inside
in that brilliant intensity
in the quiet corners of the mind,
behind that secret door into another space,
a remembered place
from a long time ago,
a comfortable place
of calm relaxation
and a deep quiet peacefulness,
a safe place to be
deep down inside,
where you may have drifted
all by yourself
quite completely at times
while I have been looking for
something to say
to help you along your way,
when all along
we both knew in some way
that it really does not matter
what I say to you,
because it all belongs to you,
to be able to let go
on the one hand
and to hold on
on the other,
the way you can hold on now
to the sensations in an arm or a leg,
to the sounds in the room,
to that feeling of awareness returning

back toward normal wakeful awareness
and drifting upwards
into a recognition
that you can let go
of where you might have been
and still hold on
to what you think
you might have learned
even as you continue
to learn more,
even as you continue
to drift up to the surface now,
up out of that trance state of mind
and into a wakeful alertness,
refreshed and rested,
and comfortably awake,
more fully awake now
than ever before
as you allow
your eyes to open
now,
that's right,
eyes open,
and the mind
wide awake
for a change,
that's right …
wide awake now!

Chapter 7

Hypnotic Surges of Energy

Although the fiery white light component of a mystical experience is the one most often described as "unbearable" in published accounts, I personally find the kinesthetic or sensory components to be the most difficult aspects of the experience to endure without flinching or disrupting the experience. The intense rush or surge of energy throughout the body that is typical of these experiences is almost more than I can bear. Riding that wave of electrified sensation as it whirls and throbs from the core of my being and pulses out through every cell with the terrifying intensity of suddenly plunging straight down into a bottomless pit requires a relaxed acceptance of imminent death, at least that is how it feels to me. It feels like being pushed off a cliff, jumping out of a plane, or riding a mile-high roller coaster.

Paradoxically, perhaps, I also find it easier to conjure up these hyper-stimulating sensations and, subsequently, find it easier to use them as an entryway into mystical types of experience than I do most of the other possible pathways. None of the other perceptual or conceptual pathways seems to have the power and clarity that kinesthetic experiences do for me. I suspect that this is because kinesthetic sensation is one of the most intense and controlling of the senses in my everyday life. It is the one that most heavily influences or even dictates the majority of my decisions and actions. Things have to "feel" right or I cannot do them and if something feels really good, I have a hard time not doing it. Whether this is the actual reason for the intensity of my reactions to kinesthetic suggestions or not, the fact remains that I am both most easily overwhelmed by and most thoroughly pleased by the types of suggestions presented in this chapter.

Although kinesthetic experiences are a minor component of the cosmic episode for many people, if you are at all kinesthetically oriented the following scripts may provide a rather challenging ride into some unusual places. At least that was my intention when

I created them. A stomach churning free-fall rush accompanied by a little underlying panic may seem like an odd place to go in search of inner peace and harmony, but paradoxically it does seem to eventually lead toward that outcome, if you can stay in your seat until the track levels out anyway.

Electrified Cells
Not everyone knows
how it feels
to pay close attention
to something being said,
to listen with your eyes closed now
as you relax deep down inside,
the way a child does
when listening to someone read
a bedtime story
full of dragons and dungeons
and magic spells galore,
or soft teddy bears
who come alive
and get up at night
and play with all the toys
when everyone else is asleep,
because some stories are easier to imagine
than others,
and it is ok right now
if you just leave your eyes closed
while you listen
to the things I am saying,
any way you want,
the same way a child does,
or not,
as long as you realize
that you have the ability to relax
much more than you know,
and you also have the ability
to allow yourself to use abilities
that you might not even know you have,
because all you really need to do now
is nothing at all for a while,

which is easy to do
because it is something you have done before,
and while doing it
you can remember
many different things
that you have done over the years
and many different things
that you have felt,
and I can imagine
that you can remember some of those things
quite clearly,
almost as if they are happening right now,
but I do not know
if you can remember
how it feels
to be suddenly shocked,
not startled or amazed
or confused or astonished
or embarrassed or surprised,
not that kind of shocked,
more like the kind of shock you feel
when you walk across a carpet
and touch a door knob
and you get that sudden jolt,
just a brief spark,
shocked just a bit,
not enough to harm you at all,
but enough to make you pull back,
or when two wires get crossed
and that electric current
goes right through a hand and an arm
and makes you jump back,
startled and surprised,
an electrifying feeling,
a shocking experience
that sends jolts of sensation
throughout the entire body,
an adrenalin surge of tingling
and a racing heart,
zapped but not killed,
a shocking surprise

to put it mildly,
or perhaps you have seen
a Van de Graaff generator,
the kind they used
in old science fiction movies,
and Frankenstein movies too,
a large metal ball
on top of a round tube,
that builds up a huge static charge
that can give off sparks
up to five-feet long
that look like lightning,
and if you put your hand on it
all your hair will stand straight up,
or if you hold a light bulb
it will light up too,
but if you are careful,
it won't hurt you
not too much anyway,
though it is thousands of volts
and that is a lot of electricity,
a lot of electrons
flowing over your skin,
and yet every sensation you feel
is the result of an electric current
flowing along bundles of nerves,
carrying an electric charge
from one place to another,
mostly up to your brain,
so that everything you hear
and everything you see
and everything you touch
is just some part of your brain
getting shocked a little bit,
getting zapped by a nerve cell
delivering a tiny electrochemical shock
to some part of the brain,
which also can be done directly
with a small electric probe,
a brief stimulation of a particular place in the brain
is all it takes to create the taste of apples

or the smell of rain
or to remind your brain
of a soft kitten
sitting in your lap
or of something bright red
that you saw the other day,
or to make a hand move,
or a leg twitch,
and so we can also wonder
what it would be like
if we could plug ourselves in
and turn up that power,
that power flowing through you,
amp up the electrons,
increase the pace of stimulation,
make all those nerves and fibers
fire faster and faster
and become more and more sensitive
until you actually become able
to feel atoms vibrating slightly
in the air next to your skin,
or hear molecules banging together
in your ears,
or able to suddenly see
photons hitting leaves
or to feel the heat waves left behind
when someone walks through a room,
the way a dog can follow smells
that we don't even know are there,
but you could recognize quite easily
after you plugged yourself in
and made every sensation
an amplification
of reality,
so that sitting there
you would become aware
of the chair supporting your weight,
without having to wait to see
if your arms
are too heavy now
to bother trying to lift,

or to recognize
that your legs are held down
by the powerful force of gravity
that even pulls your mind on down
and allows you to be aware
that this room is moving
as the earth turns,
not sitting still at all
but moving quite rapidly,
rushing to the other side
of space and time,
because each time
the earth turns
it is another day,
and this room turns too with it,
going all the way around
along with the earth
traveling that 24,000 miles around the earth
every day,
going 1,000 miles an hour
right now,
twice as fast as most airliners can go,
just by being right here now
and relaxing
and paying attention
to how it feels
to spin around that fast,
even though it may actually feel
more like you are falling,
falling forwards or backwards,
tumbling backwards and downwards,
or just floating there
in the air,
not going anywhere at all
except perhaps upwards,
because you do not really need to know
how it feels to just relax
and to not have to pay
any attention at all
to floating upwards
or floating down,

or to doing anything at all,
although I do hope you can remember
as a child
your eyes closed on a swing,
and just feeling how it felt
to swing forwards
and to swing backwards,
swinging down and back up,
back and forth,
up and down,
down and up,
or twisting the swing up
and then letting it unwind
as fast as it would go,
with your eyes closed,
paying full attention
to that spinning,
spinning around and around,
and not feeling dizzy
until the spinning stops,
and the head keeps on going
around and around,
because that is just another way
to develop a different perspective,
like hanging upside down
or looking through the wrong end
of a pair of binoculars
or a telescope,
so that everything seems
so very far away,
but what would it be like
if everything were so close
that you could just reach out in your mind
and touch it all?
What if you could feel the walls
without moving,
could feel the cars going by outside,
could feel the clouds floating past above you
or touch the rough bark of the trees,
what if you could let go
of all the edges of you,

121

no inside your skin or out,
all out and all in
at the same time,
aware of everything,
touching it all,
the walls,
the floor,
and even outdoors,
feeling currents of air moving
everywhere,
aware of soft things and hard moving
everywhere,
aware of smooth stuff and rough,
warm places and cool ones,
able to feel and taste and smell it all
all at the same time,
the way my voice
becomes just another thought of yours,
at times,
and everything else
becomes a part of you as well,
at times,
and the only thing you need to do
for now,
is to stay in touch
with how it feels
to be in touch
with all those birds
flying from place to place,
and all those animals
migrating from place to place,
and all those fish floating out there,
and all that air out there
on the Earth
floating in space,
swirling around
from place to place
with people moving through it,
allowing the mind
to touch it all,
and wonder what it all means,

even though you know
it means something even more
than you can even begin to imagine
before you begin turning that electric charge
of the mind
back down again,
calming those sensitive nerves
back down again,
letting the mind move
back down into you,
just you now for a change,
as it slows down
on the one hand
and drifts back
toward the surface of awareness
on the other hand,
back to where
you can become aware
of drifting into wakeful awareness,
now,
that's right,
more and more comfortably awake,
returning to normal wakeful awareness,
now,
back to where the eyes
can seem to open by themselves
and wakeful awareness returns
quite completely and comfortably,
that's right,
eyes open
and wide awake now.

A Rush of Emotion

As you relax there
and begin to notice
how it feels
to let go
and to surrender,
just allowing things to occur
in their own way,
at their own speed,

in their own time,
in whatever way
seems to happen automatically,
I wonder if you can notice
that falling sensation,
like falling backwards,
tumbling backwards and down,
straight down a well,
falling faster and faster at times,
going on and on,
a feeling that happens
each time you let go
and feel yourself falling faster than before,
because I know
when I let go that way
it feels just like the chair
is going out from under you,
or like a dream of falling
straight down
and in that dream
you can keep on falling and falling
while your body reacts
with a surge of sensation,
a tingling and sinking feeling
in the pit of your stomach,
a dizzy upside down tumbling
that sends shivers up your back
and makes the hairs on your neck
stand up with those tingling goose bumps
that vibrate with their own energy,
the kind of feeling that you had
the first time you looked down
off the high dive,
or over the edge of a cliff,
or heard fingernails on a blackboard,
that scraping screeching sound
that you feel everywhere
as it passes right though you,
an icy slice of sensation
right down through the middle,
from the inside out,

that tastes like cold steel
and smells like vinegar,
but with an pleasant intensity
that is hard to describe
and even harder to endure
without at least a quiver or a shiver
while trying to grab a hold
and to pull up out
of that surprising rush of feeling,
the kind of thing you feel
when someone jumps out
and yells boo
and you jump through and through
and your whole body tingles
with the energy of a surprise,
surprised by the intensity
of the feeling inside
that goes off like a flashbulb
right behind your eyes,
and how would it be
to go back to the beginning
of such an event
right back to the calm
before the surprise,
like rewinding it
and letting it happen again,
instant replay in slow motion now,
a step by step review
of that sudden intensity,
of that reaction,
of all those sensations
in that flash of surprise,
and the tingling vibration of it all,
a surging deep inside
and a ringing reverberation
in every cell,
like explosions of electricity
bursting outward,
a letting go of each piece of you
and a letting it all drift apart
into tiny atoms,

small packages of energy
coming alive
and rushing apart,
exploding outwards, faster now
and filling up the room,
filling all the space,
all the separate spaces,
filled with an instant awareness
of sensations everyplace,
of sensations all over the place
that may feel more like being tickled
than you noticed before,
a sensation that is usually felt
on the bottoms of the feet,
one foot or the other,
or under the arms,
someone held and gently touched,
touched just enough
to set off that spark,
a ticklish giggle
and curling up and pulling away
to try to get away,
but the tickling continues,
even though some people,
as you already know,
are much more ticklish
under their arms
than on their feet,
or on their stomach,
or the back of the neck,
or the back of the knee,
and how hard is it
to not let anyone know
where your most ticklish spot may be
and how parents sometimes seem to know
how to tickle you
without ever even touching you,
just wiggling their fingers next to you
and pretending that they are going to
and a child will laugh and laugh and laugh
and tell them to stop,

but as soon as it stops
they want it again,
start begging you
to do it again,
a sensation that is too much to stand,
and too good to quit,
the way many things are
when you really stop
and pay close attention to them,
the way I would like you
to pay close attention now
to your right hand and arm
to all the sensations in that right arm and hand,
right down to any feelings of warmth
or coolness in each finger,
aware of any textures,
any tingling sensations,
and of how much easier It is
to not need to bother
paying any attention at all
to the other hand and arm,
because that right arm and hand
are the only things
you really need to bother trying
to make an effort
to pay close attention to right now,
because that arm and hand know something
that you do not know yet,
but can begin to discover now
as you start to pay even closer attention
to that arm and hand
and realize how nice it would feel
to begin to notice
that hand getting bigger,
bigger and bigger,
growing,
blowing up like a balloon,
and the right arm too perhaps,
getting larger and larger,
like a big balloon
when it first begins filling up

and begins to float up,
and becomes lighter than air,
and then the right leg,
larger and larger,
more and more full
and the body as well,
filling up,
blowing up,
warm air making it all larger
and able to float in the air,
making it harder
to hold it down on the ground,
difficult to hold it back
as the whole thing
begins to float upwards,
to drift upwards into the sky
in the mind's eye,
getting larger all the time
and yet lighter and lighter as well,
light as a feather,
able to float and move
with the grace of a swan,
as light and bright
as a cloud,
stretching out
into long thin wisps of thought
that sweep across the heavens,
effortlessly filling up
all of space and time
with clouds of thought that flash and sparkle,
full of lightning and thunder now,
even though it takes some time
to realize how it feels
to be that developing storm,
becoming the winds that roar,
and the flashes of fire and thunder
from one place to another,
paying close attention now
to how it feels
when that energy begins to build,
how it feels when tiny sparks begin to fly,

getting ready to let lightning fly,
how it feels to feel that flash burst free,
how it feels to become that flash
of high power energy,
to crackle and zap from here to there
and to fill up everyplace in between
with the energy of it all,
lightning in a bottle,
all life force in a jar,
all the energy of life
and all the life of energy
right there in you,
connected to you
and you connected to it,
being all there is and ever shall be,
right here and right now,
is not something
that you will find difficult
to remember knowing about later on,
but you will find easier and easier
to discover something hidden now for you
behind that cloud,
the way rainbows always seem to hide
on the side away from the sun,
something for you to discover
and to understand now
before you continue,
something to bring back with you
to hold on to and to know
even though you also know
that you already know
something else of great importance to you,
something that can stay back down there for now,
that may drift up later on,
sometime when you least expect it,
even though now
you can continue to be aware
of how it feels
to pay close attention
to that right arm and hand of yours
and all the rest of you too,

waiting for a change now,
just resting there,
relaxed,
mind readjusting to this space out here,
the space in this room,
returning to this time,
drifting back slowly
into normal wakeful awareness now
and becoming aware of where we are
and of how it feels
to be where we are,
comfortably relaxed
and rested,
even though you may know now
that there is something you knew then
that you cannot find now
but will be there for you later on
as soon as you need it,
ready to begin to change things for you
even before you know
anything at all about it,
that's right,
even as the mind drifts upwards
and returns to the surface
of wakeful awareness now,
it is ok for you to know
that somehow you do know
there is something different here now,
different about you now,
different within you now,
easier to be more aware,
easier to be more there,
easier to just be you,
even as you open you eyes now
and return to normal wakeful awareness
now,
that's right,
comfortably wide awake
now.

Physical Sensitivities
Before you drift
into a deep trance
here now today,
I would like you first
to just sit there quietly
with your eyes closed
and relax comfortably
as you listen to me
and the things I say,
because first
I want you to find out
before you drift any deeper,
if it is possible for you
to pay close attention
to those physical sensations
on your skin
and in your muscles
and to pay attention to me
at the same time,
like being in two places
at once,
and yet not being anywhere
at all
in particular,
because most people
are very aware
of being touched,
and are very responsive
to touching soft smooth things,
or even things that are rough,
and can really enjoy
someone massaging their shoulders
or rubbing their head,
running fingers through hair,
even a gentle tickle
can be a pleasure,
and the mere pretense
of tickling a stomach,
getting closer and closer,
fingers moving in tickling ways,

can send some children
into giggles and laughter,
but not everyone
is able to actually feel
the surface of their skin very well,
not everyone can tell
how much warmer one hand is
than the other,
or which leg
seems heavier
or more relaxed
than the other,
or when that tingling sensation
seems to grow and spread
from toes
all the way up
to the top of your head,
or how your entire body
can begin to be aware
of a shivering tingle
of electrical vibrations,
tiny firings of nerve endings
along the surface of the skin
that goes on all the time,
that seem to send out flares of energy,
tiny bursts of different colored lights,
like being surrounded by fireflies
or becoming a sparkler in the night,
shooting stars off in all directions,
crackling energies getting brighter,
fields of energy like auras
charging the particles of the air,
feeling that charge build up
like becoming a battery,
so full of electricity
that sparks leap up
and fly off into space,
electrical bolts,
tiny jolts everywhere
creating a quiet roar,
all those tingling sparkles

adding together
and bursting through the skin,
lighting up the room,
illuminating the mind
and the body
from the inside out,
a neon bright tube of tingling light
with surges of energy flowing through it
in those brilliant colors
that you may be able to feel now
even easier than before,
but no one really knows
how much more fully
they can feel
some things more than others,
or how much more freely
those things will occur
as they drift more deeply
than before
and begin to really feel, now,
that particular sensation there
deep down inside, now,
the one that begins right in the center,
that ball of energy in the middle,
in the center of it all,
right in the beginning of it all,
the energy of it all
like a fiery ball
of white hot heat
that burns brightly
in the night
with a heavenly roar
of the brightest light
and yet there is more
inside than before,
and even the sound
of my voice speaking to you
can seem to be difficult
to hear over that roar
as you continue to explore
those spaces deep inside

that seem to be one thing
and turn out to be so much more,
the way that energy deep inside
connects more deeply than before
to the air out there
and the floor down there
and the air moving into you
and then out,
becoming a part of you
and then taking a part of you out with it,
the floor supporting you
and then becoming a part of you,
the earth all around you
extending out from you,
and at the center of it all
that ball of energy inside you,
like a sun within you,
a galaxy
of energies
spinning within you,
shooting out from you,
connecting to other things,
spinning around them,
becoming a part of them,
a part of other people,
of mountains and trees,
suns and moons,
attractive energies
getting stronger and stronger,
connecting everything to each other,
like magnets pulling together,
connecting it all back to you,
all moving together,
tied together
with strands of energy from you,
fields of noisy bright energy
from within you,
more powerful than before,
generating connections to it all,
reflecting connections of each to all,
until that brightness

becomes too much
to hold onto much longer,
slipping away from you
and flying outwards into space,
falling backwards in place,
tumbling backwards,
and spinning round and round,
a dizzying feeling
like winding up on a swing
and spinning round and round,
the way the earth spins round and round
each day,
each month,
and each year,
round and round goes the sun as well
and all goes round and round
everything else,
all of it orbiting
something else,
with things flying around within you
as well,
like swinging things overhead
on a long rope,
or spinning them around
and jumping a rope instead,
a rope of bright white light
full of intensely tingly energy
that comes from deep inside you
and dances on the surface
of your skin
and pulses within each muscle
of your arms and legs,
back and stomach,
right down to that churning inside,
that turning upside down
in the middle of the middle,
in the center of your stomach
and right behind your eyes
where it all comes together
in anticipation
of suddenly knowing

something that changes everything,
even though you know
that you have always known that thing
and just need to know now
that you can know now
and even know that you know
without knowing what it is
that you know now
or how to say
what you know you knew
when that energy came through you
from someplace you've never been before
and connected each to all
and all of it to you
and shot right through you,
right down into
the depths of you
where you've never been
before,
but now that you've gone on through
to the other side
of that door
you will always know
that you know something more
that is so much more
than you never knew before,
but now you do know,
although it is true
that as you begin to return
to being less aware of those things
that otherwise go overlooked
or even ignored,
you can also be aware
that you are drifting back,
back toward ordinary awareness
of just sitting there
patiently waiting
for things to calm down
and for me to say
that now you know
you can listen to the things I say

and pay close attention
to something else entirely,
like how it feels
to begin returning
to normal wakeful awareness now
where you can begin
bring back with you
a conscious memory
of those things needed
while all the rest of what happened
can stay in the background,
like a dream of things learned
on a long journey
that remain available for you
whenever you need them,
always with you
and changing things for you,
within you,
and you never know
when something else
will bubble up to the surface for you,
even after you drift back quite completely
now,
wide awake and completely rested,
refreshed and feeling quite comfortable,
as your eyes
begin to open
now
that's right,
eyes open
and wide awake now.

Roller Coasters

Very well, now,
as you relax there,
and begin to allow yourself
to feel the feeling
of letting go,
with your eyes closed,
able to listen
and able to hear

and able to understand those things needed
automatically,
with no need to make an effort,
no need to try
to do anything at all for a while
because it is just so much easier
to just allow yourself
to drift down now,
to let go now,
and to allow
a light trance,
a deep trance,
a deeper trance to develop
over time
even as you reach the entrance
to that place,
a place you may have been before,
a place in the mind,
a restful place
where you can explore,
quite comfortably now,
whatever occurs along the way
as you allow
that comfortable trance
to continue to develop,
to become a part of your experience
or to become all of your experience
with each breathing in
and each breathing out,
and thinking about
those things that occur
deep down inside
where deep thoughts hide
and you can follow that path
that leads down into that place,
deep down inside the mind,
because the mind
has many different levels,
many different layers,
like the layers of rock
or the rings of a tree,

created over the years,
over the centuries,
over the ages,
each age a new layer,
each stage a new level,
a new level of understanding,
a new level of learning,
learning about something
not known about before,
or more about something
known forevermore,
and learning how much more
there is to know
about how to drift down
to those levels down below,
to let go of the outside now
and to drift down into the inside
and to enter into a place,
a quiet space deep down inside,
a safe place to hide,
a place where you can go
to relax and let go,
and to feel that heaviness
as arms relax,
and hands relax,
and fingers relax,
and legs relax,
and shoulders relax,
and even the back relaxes
as the neck relaxes
and the face relaxes,
and then the stomach relaxes
while the chest relaxes,
and the feet relax,
even the eyes relax,
and can ears relax
while the mind relaxes as well,
or can they relax even more than the rest,
the way some people can relax
even more than the rest
when a roller coaster ride begins

and the chains jerk things forward,
each car bumping forward,
jumping a bit forward,
one, two, and three,
rolling forward,
and beginning that climb,
going up that steep incline,
pulled up higher and higher
where you can begin looking around now
at all the sights and sounds
of everything going on all around
way down below,
but not everyone knows
how to relax along the way,
how to feel peace settling in
deep down inside
as the roller coaster keeps going higher
and getting closer to the top,
and getting ready to drop
straight down on the other side,
which is the exact moment
when some people
start holding on really tight,
and scrunch up their faces
and squish their eyes closed,
and hold their breath,
and their stomach starts churning,
and they begin being terrified
that they are going to die,
while at exactly the same time,
sitting right next to them,
other riders begin to smile,
to let go of the bar,
to hold their arms straight up in the air
and to begin laughing and yelling "Hurray!",
looking forward to the fall
with increasing joy and excitement,
laughing out loud as the cars plunge straight down
then fly around a corner
and turn upside down
and twist around for a while,

while those people keep laughing,
knowing somewhere deep inside,
that it is all just a dream here now,
an imagined event,
where you can fly away
any time you want,
just put out your arms,
and jump over the side,
flying off someplace else
going deeper into a trance
then letting go of more and more
and finding it easier and easier
to just allow things to happen,
to allow the unconscious mind
to assume more and more
responsibility
for taking care of those things needed,
so that all you need to do,
is nothing at all,
just sitting back,
and going along for the ride,
going down deep inside,
where you can be aware,
but do not need to try
to do anything there,
the way you can be aware
of those sensations down there,
somewhere deep inside,
trapped in a bubble,
contained in a cloud,
unreachable right now
but beginning to grow,
beginning to develop
into something big,
something bigger than before,
like the tiny excitement
of a growing surprise,
something getting closer and closer,
knowing something is coming
but not knowing what,
something unknown,

something hidden,
something secret,
kept deep inside all this time
starting to break free
and to drift up into awareness,
getting bigger and closer,
a secret surprise feeling,
like looking forward to a gift,
a present for one and all
behind a door
in the back of the mind
that you can find now
and unwrap now
and discover what it is,
because there are many things
that you want
but is exactly what you need,
including tickets for a new ride,
a better ride,
that furiously flies
with an increasing roar
straight down toward a pool
of brilliant white fire
full of pulsating heat
that blasts right though you,
vaporizes you,
turns you into
light floating free,
light coming out
and streaming away
in all directions,
filling that space,
all space and time,
with your own mind,
the light of your mind
in infinite space,
infinite mind filling that space
with an awareness
that you are here
and everywhere
at the same time

but also nowhere as well,
and your ability to ride those waves
of electrified sensation
throughout your entire body,
out to the very edge of it all,
is the same ability
that lets you hear the sun with your skin,
touch the stars with your eyes,
move the earth with a twitch,
and I wonder now
if you can remember a time
when you could smell new mown grass
or hear crickets singing
and get lost for a time
in the softness of fur,
and I wonder as well
if you can imagine
how it will feel
to remember
something that will happen
next week
or perhaps tomorrow,
when that feeling of falling
on that brand new ride
down into that bright fiery light
in the middle of your mind
returns to remind you
of something deep inside
that remained behind
when all else disappeared,
something never-ending
in the center of it all,
something you share
with the creation of it all
that stays with you
no matter where you go
or what you forget to remember,
it stays there as a part of it all,
connected to everything you are,
everything you do,
everything you ever will be or do,

because it all belongs to you
and it goes right on through
like a raindrop
falling back into the ocean,
down into the waves,
into the source
where it all began,
just as we began today
with a letting go
and a drifting into a comfortable relaxation,
and now you can begin to drift upwards again,
back into a refreshing state of wakeful awareness
where being there,
aware of your arms,
and aware of your legs,
and aware of the sounds in the room,
is as easy as allowing yourself
to realize that your eyes
can begin to feel
like they are going to open soon,
and the mind can return
to normal wakeful awareness soon,
where the body will feel rested
and things feel fine
even as the eyes
are allowed to open
now ...
that's right,
eyes open
and returning to wakeful awareness
now.

Chapter 8

Hypnotic Reverberations of Sound

As a second year graduate student I spent an entire summer working all day seeing clients in a counseling center some days and patients in a mental hospital the rest of the week. When I got home I was already physically tired and mentally exhausted but I was convinced that I needed to study for my upcoming comprehensive doctoral exam for several hours every evening if I hoped to finish the reading list and pass the exam that fall semester. Out of sheer necessity, therefore, and purely by chance, I devised a way of relaxing at the end of the day that that allowed me to rest and recuperate relatively fully within only 20 to 30 minutes.

Before I did anything after I got home, before even fixing something to eat, I put an album on my cheap stereo, lay down on the couch, put on headphones, and drifted off into the sounds of classical arrangements by Bach or Beethoven and of late 60s groups such as the Doors or the Beatles. I always chose something fairly mellow because I wanted to relax, but I also gravitated toward fairly complex arrangements because they were more engrossing. Complex arrangements allowed me to pay attention to one instrument at a time or one voice at a time and, by shifting from one to another as the record played, to build up an appreciation for the overall pattern of relationships between all of these sounds.

At some point very early that summer I began trying to "feel" the sound and rhythm of one instrument or voice in one part of my body and the sound and rhythm of another instrument or voice in another part of my body. This was an incredibly absorbing experience; it required a great deal of attention, it was unusual and pleasurable, and it also allowed me to forget about everything else entirely. My body became the music, the band, or the orchestra. When one side of an album was over and the record player stopped, I felt a sudden rush of sensation, automatically snapped out of it, opened my eyes, and emerged feeling quite refreshed.

In hindsight I can now see that this simple relaxation exercise also was a transformational experience for me personally in some ways. I became more comfortable, more relaxed, and more attuned to the patterns of sounds and sights around me. Without intending to do so or even realizing at the time that I was doing so, I now believe that I was simulating a meditative experience. I had not yet become interested in mediation or cosmic consciousness, but I was nonetheless regularly generating brief episodes of relaxed integrative awareness at an auditory and a kinesthetic level. By learning how to feel like I was becoming the harmonies and rhythms of the music, I also was becoming more harmoniously in tune with integrative patterns within myself and the world around me.

It is possible that this summer of musical reverie set the stage for my subsequent interest and involvement in meditation and mystical consciousness. If nothing else, it set the stage for the scripts presented in this particular chapter. Their structure and content is derived directly from that summer of late afternoon meditative listening sessions. I doubt that the harmonies of John, Paul, George, and Ringo are in the same class as the celestial harmonies of a mystical episode, but much of their work seemed cosmic to me at the time and, I have to admit, most of it still does.

A Chorus of Angels
Now I want you to know,
as you begin to let your eyes close
and arrange yourself there
so you are very comfortable,
arms and hands relaxed,
mind and body relaxed
and able to pay close attention,
that there is no absolutely right way
and no absolutely wrong way
to enter into a trance here today,
a relaxed state of mind
where your eyes can be closed
quite comfortably now
and you can be

quite comfortable now
and you can listen
to all the different things I might say
quite comfortably now,
while you continue to be aware
of your own internal events
those thoughts and sensations
in hands and arms,
legs and feet,
as the body relaxes
and the mind shifts into
a different state of mind,
a relaxed awareness
of a quiet trance
that can continue to develop
and become deeper and deeper
over time,
and that's fine,
and all you need to do
while you rest there
with your eyes closed
listening to me,
and begin to continue
to relax fully,
and to consider
that the human voice
has been used for centuries
for so much more
than talking like I am doing
to you here and now,
or for laughing out loud,
or for loudly yelling,
or even quietly chanting,
but for singing,
alone and with others,
in imitation of birds,
those angelic beings
that soar through the air
on feathered wings
and sing complex songs
from rooftops and fields,

from treetops and clouds,
to attract attention
to call a mate,
to simply announce,
I was here first,
this space belongs to me,
singing back and forth to each other,
answering each other
or singing at each other,
competing to impress someone else,
but I have never heard of a bird
singing in harmony with another,
singing with another,
or a group of others
the way people do,
the way we imagine
angels do,
soaring through heaven,
on feathered wings,
playing harps and singing
in a heavenly chorus,
like an earthly choir,
wearing robes instead of wings,
sounds blending together,
voices adding together,
becoming one huge sound
that fills a room,
and fills the mind
and invites you to join,
to sing around that sound,
to hear that sound surround
the mind and body
the way you have heard before,
the way you have felt before,
and that reminds me
of a particular episode of a TV program
on PBS
called *Great Performances*
that featured Paul McCartney
playing in a small club setting
where the stage was full

of many different instruments,
drums, pianos, guitars of all sorts,
even a large bass and a synthesizer,
and in the course of that program
he played each instrument
while singing a song he had written,
and each rendition was perfect and beautiful,
and at the end
he had the audience provide melodies
that he played on one instrument or another
while a sound engineer recorded each one,
and when they were all played back together,
they all blended together
to make a delightful song
that Paul made up words to
and then got the audience to sing along too,
so that by the end
everyone was singing all together
a song they had created together
with a sound that seemed like a celestial choir,
and I wonder if you can remember
the most beautiful choir
you have ever heard,
the beauty and power
of all that energy,
of all those harmonies
soaring with the score
as they blend together more and more,
and do you realize,
sitting here now,
wondering about hearing now,
how long has it been
since you have listened,
really listened,
to a sound like that
with your eyes closed,
like they are now,
and you listened,
with your ears opened,
like they are now,
and you began to allow

your mind to really hear that music,
those instruments,
the sound of those voices
arranging themselves together,
flowing and weaving together
the way water flows all together,
each source a small stream
flowing into others,
flowing all together
and getting bigger and wider
and rushing toward the edge
of that huge waterfall,
higher than the sky,
wider than the imagination,
plunging down with a roar,
all sounds together in that roar,
the sound of every voice
in perfect harmony,
because you know how it sounds
as you move closer and closer
when approaching a waterfall,
hearing that huge full sound,
all those sounds at once,
a roaring rush of sound
that gets louder and louder
as you get closer and closer,
close enough to finally
begin to actually feel it,
to feel that sound vibrate
the bones of your chest,
and rattle the depths of your mind,
playing with the imagination,
a sound that surrounds the mind
with the hum of loud voices,
the depth of a pipe organ,
the intensity of an orchestra
all playing at once,
that crescendo of sound
that comes toward the end
that announces the end,
the grand finale,

but it is not the end
and it is just the beginning
of one hallelujah after another
that goes on and on,
on and on,
building and building,
hour after hour,
day after day,
forever and ever
without beginning or end
getting louder and louder,
moment after moment,
a sound you can feel
from your feet
to your chest
to the middle of your mind,
as if you are singing it,
as if your body is creating it,
as if the vibrations
are coming from you,
as if you are it
yourself,
a sound coming from you
a sound becoming you,
becoming all you feel,
becoming all you hear,
becoming all you are,
a heavenly harmony
of sounds that are you
and everything else too,
here and now,
as you allow that sound
to move through you,
surrendering to it,
allowing it
to wash right over you,
to wash you away
over that edge,
the edge of that falls,
plunging into that roar,
into that sound

of an angels' chorus,
of all sounds at once,
together in perfect harmony,
as if the world itself
is singing to you,
singing through you
to all the other worlds
in the universe,
matching their sounds,
harmonizing with them,
a celestial chorus,
a harmony of the heavens,
singing to each other,
attracting attention,
looking for a mate
announcing love
and making connections,
each to the other,
a feeling that echoes
in the back of the mind,
a realization that continues
even as you realize while sitting there
that you can follow
the sound of my voice
back into this room
back into here and now,
and begin to return
to wakeful awareness,
gradually waking up now,
becoming more fully awake and alert,
where your eyes begin to feel like opening,
and the mind begins to feel
refreshed and aware,
aware of being there,
right there,
comfortably aware,
and comfortably awake now,
as your eyes open now,
and the mind awakens as well,
that's right,
comfortably wide awake now.

Zen Chants

You can now close your eyes,
and relax for a while,
while I wonder
if you have ever heard
a recording of Zen monks
chanting "Om" together,
or better yet,
a recording of one Zen monk
singing Om in harmony
with himself,
which sounds impossible,
I know,
because everyone knows,
that the human voice
makes just one sound
at a time
and harmony requires many different sounds
all at once,
different parts of a musical scale
blending together,
vibrating together,
pulsating the air together
in waves of sound energy,
waves that rebound around
and enter the ear and
move into the mind
all at the same time
where we can hear
those relationships blend together,
harmonize with one another,
amplify and justify each other,
but one voice at a time
usually does not sing
in perfect harmony
with itself,
and yet why not,
because who else knows
better than you
exactly when
you begin to hear

one sound
and stop hearing another,
which is exactly why
we can wonder
what the sound is
of one hand clapping
and why we can wonder
what the sound is
of one voice harmonizing
with itself,
which is only worth wondering
if you have not heard it
because if you have heard it being done
then you no longer wonder,
you just know
that it really is true,
that there are monks
who do this very thing,
sing harmony with themselves,
and sometimes they chant
with others doing it too
so that just a few
can sound like hundreds
and fill a room with sound,
a booming bass vibration of
"Oooooommmmmm"
that seems to just go on and on,
like the sound of a gong
or the waves coming in
over and over
on top of each other,
and what would it be like
to sing all the parts
all at once like that
of a huge choir,
a chorus of voices
all the same person
singing at all of it
all at once,
and how would that feel,
to be able to feel

all that sound
coming out of you,
how does it feel
to open your mind
to the possibility
of how it would sound
to sing all those voices
at the same time,
something you can feel
in your own mind
in the same way
that you can feel
how it would feel
if you could hear
each cell in your body
vibrate with sound,
all the different sounds
they are making right now,
thousands and millions
of sounds all at once,
all those atoms
banging around,
connecting to each other,
all at the same time
going on and on across time,
a sound so powerful
it can vibrate the ground,
shake the trees,
rattle buildings,
captivating everyone
the world around,
who, upon hearing that sound
coming from you,
from everywhere within you,
would all turn around,
and begin hearing that sound,
and sending out their own sound
from deep, deep down in each cell
already rumbling around
within the center of them as well,
a sound from the center of it all,

where it all began,
that sound of it all beginning again,
a sound
that can now be found
within your own mind,
within your own body,
within each cell of you
as you listen carefully
and hear it too,
right there,
vibrating throughout you
in tune with the sound
of the sun shining
and the stars moving
and things beginning to be,
in tune with everything moving everywhere
even the particles of the air,
moving with that sound
and the sound of a sunset
or the rising of a full moon,
the sound of flowers blooming
and a thought taking time
to consider the beginning
of everything happening
all at once
all the time
in a dance,
a coordinated movement,
a movement of sound
that orchestrates it all,
that comes from it all
and is it all
and is all there is there,
a sound creating it all
and being created by it all
now ...
and then
after a while
being here again
being now again
and bringing with you

whatever part of that sound
you want or need to keep with you
and able to remember it
as you drift back
into wakeful awareness now,
like drifting out of a dream
where some things,
and not others,
drift back with you
but knowing,
even as your eyes begin to open
now,
and the mind returns
to wakeful awareness
with those things
that are useful to you,
now,
that's right,
knowing that you can
become fully awake
and fully aware
quite comfortably now,
that's right,
fully aware of
returning to wakeful awareness
quite completely
now.

The Vibration of Atoms

You have the ability now
to close your eyes slowly
and to begin to relax comfortably,
that's right,
eyes closed now,
comfortably relaxing,
but you do not have the ability
to close your ears
and so they continue to hear
even after you stop making the effort
to pay close attention
to everything I say

and the sound of my voice
will go with you everywhere
as you drift from place to place
like the sound of the wind in the trees
or the murmur of voices in the background
as you continue to drift down
into a light trance
or a deep trance
and that is just fine,
because it really does not matter
how deeply down into a trance
your mind goes now,
because your ears
are continuing to hear
and your mind
continues to understand
that what your mind hears
is just a small part of what is being said,
and what the ears hear
is just a small part
of what is being done out there,
all that activity everywhere
all around,
with clouds moving around
and wind blowing,
with leaves shaking
and raindrops falling
with thunder in the background,
and the sound of matches striking
to light candles in the night
or logs in the fireplace
that snap, crackle, and pop,
altogether it all
makes a buzzing background of sound,
while further down
beneath the surface of the mind
where no one ever really stops
to listen carefully,
really deep, deep down,
further down than the sound
of sand crunching

or water flowing,
further down than the sound
of ice melting
or water boiling
further down than cells growing
or the mind talking to itself,
down into the sounds electrons make
when they bump into each other,
a banging around rattling sound,
down into the sounds of light
streaming through a window
hitting everything inside,
bouncing all around the room
like a pinball machine,
even filling the corners with photons
banging around
scattering light everywhere,
but how does it sound
to your finely tuned ear
to hear atoms vibrating
like tiny tuning forks,
singing with energy
all around us everywhere,
each reacting
to all the other sounds,
the way a violin reacts
to the sound of another violin being played,
sympathetic vibrations,
things vibrating together,
like crickets and tree frogs
filling the woods with sound,
only this sound in you
goes all around everywhere all the time,
even the atoms in your body,
each finger tip
humming with sound,
the way it feels
to rub the wet rim of a glass
to make it hum and sing with sound
and I wonder if you can hear it
as you begin to feel it

vibrating from head to toe,
and in the air as well,
all of it full of sound,
atoms singing out loud,
spilling their energy
into your ears
and into your mind,
so many different sounds
than you hear every day,
the sounds of the air
touching the skin,
the sound of light
hitting a wall,
the sound of the sun,
a constant roar,
a nuclear fire,
a ball of energy
that we can feel and see
but cannot hear from here,
and yet deep inside,
with the eyes closed,
the roar of that sun
can be felt,
and that light
can be seen,
a bright light,
a speck of light so bright
down deep inside the mind
that it slips out of sight at first,
then comes back into awareness
a bit better than before,
caught by the energy of that roar
where it can be heard a bit clearer,
can be felt a bit more
as you relax and notice
that the mind moves down toward it
automatically,
each time you let go
it becomes easier
to be more aware of it,
to notice more of it,

to see and feel it more clearly,
to hear that energy roar,
the roar of a lion,
the roar of a bear,
nothing compares
to the sound of that place in you,
deep down inside,
giving off all that light,
giving off all that heat,
and yet there is so much more
to hear down there,
down where it all begins
to flow into awareness
after the dams let go
and the flow becomes easier
and the mind floods with light
stored up in deep spaces,
a flow of energy,
of electrons moving from place to place,
banging into each other like tiny bells,
singing sounds like wind chimes,
signifying movement of thought
instead of wind,
a sound that can be felt
in every cell in the body,
in every thought of the mind,
a sound that becomes a chorus,
children's voices blending together,
mothers and fathers joining in,
singing something deeply moving,
the sound of all sounds everywhere
heard through headphones
in the middle of the mind,
a sound of songs and hymns,
of laughter and surprise,
a sound of different shapes and sizes,
of different colors and textures,
and even when you begin to wonder
if you even understand
what it is that is happening to you
or what is being said to you

or what it all might mean,
you already know
that there are sounds
that can be heard around the world,
and many animals communicate
in ways that cannot be heard,
elephants have a rumble
that reverberates for miles,
and whales can say hello
from one ocean to another,
and porpoises can use sound
to see inside each other
and to see their food as well,
and the sounds we feel
inside ourselves
also can reveal much more
than we knew was there,
even tell us
where we have been before
and where we might be going later on,
but for now
the only thing you need to know
is that you already do know
that your sound judgment
can be based on the sounds you hear
as well as the sounds that you do not,
and so as we begin to continue to explore
all those things heard and heard about,
I would like you to know
about something I heard about,
a computer program
that connects to a video camera
and changes images into sound
that allows people who cannot see
to learn to hear what things look like
and to experience the world
in a new and different way,
and so here today,
I would like you to have an opportunity
to experience even more about how it feels
to hear how things look

and to see things with sound,
to feel things with sound
and to hear the way things feel,
to hear the sound of things all around,
the sound of things being,
and to be the sound of things all around,
to let the mind hear the way the world sounds
and whirl away with the sound of the galaxy,
hear the sound of the mind breaking free
and becoming all sounds everywhere,
and then to letting it all come back together again,
feel it collapsing back into you,
pulling it all in,
and becoming it all again,
with ears wide open,
and the eyes wide shut,
feeling the mind drifting back,
aware of being here now,
of the mind slowly drifting up again,
returning to ordinary wakeful awareness again,
gradually and comfortably
moving out of that trance
and waking up now
more and more completely
until eventually
the eyes can be allowed to begin to open
and the mind can be allowed
to begin to awaken as well,
and then a deep breath,
that's right,
more and more awake,
more and more aware of arms and legs,
and another deep breath now,
that's right,
and then eyes open now,
that's right,
and wakeful awareness returns completely,
that's right,
wide wake,
Now.

Chapter 9

Hypnotic Awareness of Perfection

There is an intellectual or cognitive component to the cosmic consciousness experience that centers on an understanding and appreciation of perfection in the form of perfect harmony, perfect order, perfect symmetry, perfect logic, perfect performance, or perfect design. This aspect of the experience is usually described as an outgrowth of a mystical event rather than as the trigger of such events. At times, however, an insight into the perfection of something, almost anything, can prompt a transformational surge into a peak experience.

Nature is a typical source of perceived perfection. Examples include the spiral beauty of a seashell, the glory of a sunset, the fragile wonder of butterfly wing, the magic of a snowflake, and the miniature perfection of a newborn's hand. And many peak experiences actually happen on mountain peaks.

Artistic creations are another common source. One of my early peak experiences occurred while examining a copy of Rodin's *The Cry* in the Oberlin College Art Museum. I was taking a sculpture class there at the time and I stopped to examine this piece to see how Rodin had managed to capture the human body, something I definitely had not been able to do in my class. As I walked around this evocative rendition of a nude young man kneeling, his arm outstretched toward the heavens, his mouth open in a passionate scream, my first thought was that everything was wrong with this sculpture.

One arm was longer than the other, the upper arm was too short, the face was distorted, and the muscles of the back were all in the wrong places. Nothing was as it "should" be and yet that sculpture was a perfect representation of a man screaming at and imploring the heavens. Everything was as it had to be to convey the emotion underlying that event. As soon as I fully realized this, it was as if something exploded in my brain. I was overwhelmed by the perfection of this work, awestruck by it. I lost track of time as I walked around and around it, dumbfounded by the genius of the artist, joyful in the discovery of a truth I did not know exactly how to express then and still do not know how to express now. All I know is that I had never before seen or understood the perfection of something that was so obviously imperfect.

Perfection, like beauty, is in the eye of the beholder. A rose can seem perfect to one person and quite flawed to another. A sophisticated mathematical formula may seem perfect to those who understand it and merely puzzle the rest of us. Perfection is subjective and rare from some points of view but to those who enter into a mystical state it becomes an inherent aspect of every component of the universe, even down to each grain of sand. Thus, the scripts presented in this chapter encourage the acceptance and awareness of perfection as an entryway into cosmic consciousness. For some people this may represent a significant and initially uncomfortable departure from a more critical or analytic perspective. Others may find it to be a familiar and reassuring attitude. Either way, allowing oneself to become experientially connected to internal and/or external perfections can move the mind into some fascinating spaces.

Purification

To begin with today
I would like to have you
hold both hands out in front of you,
palms up,
that's right,
arms suspended in the air,
both hands in front of you,
palms up
as if you are holding something,
a bowl perhaps,
something smooth and round
but very light,
and as you close your eyes now
you can pay closer attention
to how it feels

to hold that object there,
up in the air a bit,
as light as a cloud
or a balloon,
and over time
as you pay close attention to it
you may notice
that you can imagine
someone filling it with water,
pouring water into it,
making it heavier and heavier
even as you relax inside
more and more
and drift down deeper and deeper,
entering a quiet trance,
an effortless state
of relaxed awareness,
like those who participate
year after year
in a solemn ritual,
a purification ritual
while holding a bowl
as water is poured into it,
purified water perhaps,
so that everything it touches
becomes pure as well,
and as that bowl gets heavier
and heavier
it really is ok now
to allow your hands to move down
more and more,
as that bowl seems to become
heavier and heavier in your mind
arms drifting down slowly,
gradually moving down
until that bowl
and your hands
can come to rest in your lap,
that's right,
gradually moving down
that way now

and then allowing your hands
to rest relaxed and comfortable
in your lap now,
while a quiet calmness
continues in the purity
of the background
and you can become aware
that you are sitting there
listening to me here
talking about purifications with water,
baptisms and such,
all with water,
a substance pure enough to cleanse the soul,
pure enough to see right through,
clear as air,
so pure and clear
that when it becomes clear to you
that a dish needs to be cleaned
you use water to do it,
do you not,
and when hands need to be cleaned
you use water to do it,
do you not,
and when the body
needs to be cleaned
you use water to do it,
don't you,
cleaned and purified
from the outside in
and from the inside out
so that when you drink it in
it becomes a part of you,
flows into you
and purifies you,
a substance so pure
it can wash away dusty sins
the way rain washes away dust
and smoothes out the tracks
that deer leave behind
as they walk through a field
searching for food

leaving behind footprints
and taking with them
everything they need,
because nature provides
for all those creatures,
provides whatever they need,
food, shelter and water
in a perfect balance,
a harmony of creation
that is easily ignored,
easily overlooked,
because it all just keeps on going
the way the water just keeps on flowing,
automatically,
moving down and around everything,
automatically,
becoming streams and rivers
and flowing outwards to the seas
where nature provides
for all those creatures as well,
provides everything they need
in a perfect balance
that keeps them going
generation after generation,
following the same routes
from one place to another,
eating and growing,
the way every cell in your body
continues to grow
and to absorb nutrition
from the blood that flows
outwards into arms and legs
and back into the heart,
back into the heartland,
the center of it all,
back where it all begins
and where it all becomes
pure and free,
washed in the filters
of a spring that flows
from deep inside

with that clear cool water
that fills the caves
and bubbles up to the surface
cool and clean
bringing with it
the salts and minerals required
to build strong bones eight ways,
filled with calcium
that used to be a rock
deep down in the ground,
now dissolved in that water
poured into that bowl
that we are using here today
to purify your mind,
to wash it clear and clean
with its perfect clarity
and its perfect purity,
pure perfection
of design and execution,
like the gymnast's perfect ten score
while performing on the parallel bars,
every movement graceful and sure,
every moment an artistic creation,
like a sculpture moving
from one position to another,
each position exactly right,
just as perfect
as the one before,
but different,
the way each leaf is perfect
but different from all the rest,
or the perfect beauty of a face,
or the playful perfection of a kitten,
all different
but all still perfect at the same time,
the way bells can ring clear and clean,
each one a perfect tone
but each one different,
and when rung together,
a harmony of perfections
from one end of the scale to the other,

a sound from deep within,
church bells and chapel bells,
doorbells and sleigh bells,
bells that announce new beginnings
and bells that toll recent endings,
with a solemn power that carries a sound
for miles and miles all around,
a sound that you can feel
vibrating in your mind,
that one perfect tone
that is your tone, your sound,
the harmonious sound that you would be
if you were a bell,
or could hear the sound of your cells
humming together in perfect harmony,
a sound that makes the water vibrate
in that bowl on your lap,
makes the ripples flow
across its surface
but does not change its purity
or alter your perfection,
but lets you know quite well
exactly how it feels
to have your own impurities washed away,
to have imperfections eliminated,
to become as pure and clear
as the purest water anywhere,
to accept and to understand
fully and completely,
if only for a moment,
that you are, at that moment,
perfectly pure and clean,
exactly perfect
and just what you are supposed to be,
perfect just the way you are
from deep inside in the darkest secret places
all the way out to the surface,
as perfect as a flower,
as perfect as a rainbow,
as perfect as anything can be
or ever will be

and you always will be,
no matter what,
and that's that,
is it not?
So just for an instant,
just a second perhaps,
it really is ok
to allow yourself to know
what you knew for sure as a child
and still believe in there somewhere,
that you really are ok,
perfect in every way,
and that is why now
you can take that leap
and enter that space
where it really is ok
to believe it in every way,
just for a moment is fine,
no matter what other thoughts
may come your way,
you can brush them away
and know that it is ok,
at least for right now,
that's right,
to be aware of that perfection
that is you,
at least right now,
and always will be,
that's right,
even though it might be difficult
to hold on to that thought completely
later on,
even after you start drifting up now
toward the surface of wakeful awareness
where you can allow some of it
to drift back with you, perhaps,
like drops of that pure water
held in that round bowl
that poured clear through your soul
and washed you clean
and left behind some drops of purity,

some memories of that place,
some pieces of that feeling
to bring back with you now,
even as you continue
to drift back into
wakeful awareness now,
that's right,
drifting back up to the surface,
aware of arms and legs,
of the sounds in this room,
like waking up from a deep sound sleep,
feeling comfortably rested and refreshed,
more and more wide awake,
until it is quite comfortable now
to allow the eyes to open
and wakeful awareness to return,
that's right,
eyes open,
and wide awake now!

The Clearing
Our goal here today
is to help you
enter into a trance,
a light trance
or a deep trance,
just a comfortably relaxed
entranced state of mind,
where you can listen
to the things I say
and allow the mind to drift along
with the sounds of my words,
the way we all listened
to a story as a child
with our eyes closed
while someone read
the words out loud
and we had our eyes closed
and our mind open,
the way your eyes can be closed now,
relaxing and listening,

and your mind can be open,
waiting to find out
what happens next,
without trying to do anything at all,
just letting the mind's eye follow along
wherever the story goes,
which is just another way of saying
that you do not need to try
to do anything at all
for a while,
and you certainly do not need to try
to do a trance perfectly,
or to do a perfect trance,
because it is so much easier
to just let perfection happen
without even noticing or trying,
the way perfection happens all the time
all around us,
easily overlooked, but there
in everything we examine closely,
like the cells of a leaf,
perfectly formed,
perfectly designed,
to be exactly where they are,
the way the leaves of trees
on the edge of a woods
are designed to let the wind through
but the leaves of trees,
the same type of trees,
in the middle of a forest,
where there is much less wind
are fatter and bigger
to absorb more sunlight
which is less available
in the middle of all that shade
than on the edge where the sun shines,
or the shape of flowers
that are beautiful enough
the way we see them
but also have complex designs
we cannot see,

their petals have colors
our eyes cannot detect,
but insects can,
they can see those bright
ultraviolet centers
inviting them in
where pollen can be found,
or other flowers designed
for just one insect,
designed to deposit
a package of pollen
on that one bee,
a bee that survives
on the nectar from that one flower,
the only bee
that can even get into it,
a perfect design,
all the way around,
and some people think
that such things are unusual,
that perfect designs are rare
or that only human beings
can do something perfectly,
that only people are smart enough
to figure things out,
when the fact is
that everything else
does everything perfectly
and only people fall short,
because their effort to be perfect
is bound to fail in some ways
since perfection only occurs
without effort, without thought,
ice crystals are perfect examples,
and so are clouds,
and birds soaring,
and leopards leaping,
and so you do not need to try
to enter a perfect trance,
or to do anything perfectly
for a while,

not even nothing at all,
no one can do nothing perfectly,
because whatever happens automatically
is the only perfection you need for now
and being able to allow whatever occurs
to happen on its own is hard enough to do
without having to try to do
anything else at all,
because after all
a ray of light does not have to try
to turn into a rainbow
and a drop of water
does not have to try
to fall from the sky
any more than the Earth itself
has to try to circle the sun
at exactly the right distance,
in just the right way,
to create night and day,
and the seasons as well,
no effort involved at all,
things just happen that way,
that perfect way,
exactly the way
it has to be,
perfect harmony of design and function,
so while you relax there
and allow a trance to develop
on its own,
I can wonder if you
have ever seen something perfect,
heard something that sounded perfect
learned something that blew your mind
understood something that amazed you
because it was so perfectly obviously true,
or watched a perfection happen,
right before your eyes,
an event that you still hold dear,
an experience that you treasure,
the one thing
that you want to remember

after everything else
has faded away,
that perfect moment
of that perfect day,
and the way
it felt
to realize
how beautifully perfect it was,
how perfect it still is for you
deep down inside,
sitting in there,
a cornerstone,
an event that defines
everything else,
a moment in time and space
that you may not have thought about
for a long, long time,
but can drift back into awareness now
from behind those clouds,
or maybe it is something you remember
each and every day,
something you keep with you
every moment
because you know now
that it changed everything for you,
because once you saw it,
once you experienced that moment so pure,
once you felt everything shift into place,
the beauty of that truth
and the truth of that beauty
spreads out to everything,
and begins to bring
something new to you,
newborn to you,
so fresh and true,
a perfect moment,
perfect for you,
a memorable event,
and the warmth of that time,
the feel of that place,
like the strength of a child's hug,

or the clear coolness of a breeze
on top of a mountain
looking out for miles and miles and miles,
or the soft freshness of a new kiss
and the joy of a hearty laugh,
the depth of loving eyes,
there is perfection everywhere,
and so I wonder
where are yours kept,
your perfect moments,
those precious times,
not just memories,
but instant understandings,
admissions about yourself,
allowing yourself to know
that it really is true
that things in life are perfect at times,
and you are perfect too
in so many ways,
when you look into your eyes,
and listen to your thoughts,
hearing what you know,
accepting what you see,
and remembering,
that you can find heaven
in a grain of sand,
a mustard seed,
a baby's hand,
a lover's smile,
the rings of Saturn
the redness of Mars,
or the man in the moon
on a full moon night
with a sky full of stars,
and looking up at it all,
feeling so small,
in the vastness of it all,
and finally realizing
just how many stars there are
and how very far away,
how infinite it really is,

how infinitely incredible,
and yet the perfection of it all
belongs to you,
that perfection is within you,
that perfection that is you,
and all around you too,
so as you sit there,
aware of it all,
of not needing to try
to do anything at all,
you can wonder
what part of this all
you can keep with you
as you let go of it all
and drift back here now,
drifting into a wakeful awareness
of everything around you, now,
back to this room, now,
back to my voice, now,
back to the surface
of ordinary wakeful awareness
bringing with you
all those things
that belong to you,
keeping them close to you,
a part of you,
even as you continue
back to the surface now,
quite completely,
where your eyes can open
now ...
that's right,
eyes open
and comfortably
wide awake now.

Truth and Beauty
Ok,
let's begin
by having you
close your eyes today

so that you can pay close attention
to the things I might say
without being distracted
by all the things around the room
and at the same time
pay closer attention
to your own thoughts and sensations,
like all those different sensations
that might go overlooked
in a hand, or an arm,
a slight tingling sensation perhaps,
that seems to grow and spread,
as you relax,
and a feeling of heaviness begins,
and you become more and more relaxed
and able to pay closer and closer attention
to the idea
that things can seem to be different
but turn out to be the same,
the way truth and beauty
seem to be two different things at first,
but turn out to be the same,
with truth being beautiful
and beauty being truthful,
and that is just one example among many,
because our purpose here today
is to give you an opportunity
to discover even more
about the way things seem
when you allow yourself
to pay close attention
without wondering
if that is the way
they are supposed to be,
which is really a very different notion
from the traditional idea
that things must be arranged
to be just right,
must be organized and orderly
to be appealing,
like the formal gardens

of European palaces,
every plant lined up
and evenly spaced,
all arranged in squares and circles,
geometric patterns everywhere,
with bushes trimmed into spheres and blocks,
some even formed into the shapes of animals,
and trees flattened up against a wall,
espaliered they call it,
like a soldier standing there,
shoulders back against the wall,
standing stiff and tall,
not like a tree at all,
order imposed on the chaos of nature
in the ongoing search for beauty,
which is a very different style
from the gardens of Japan,
where the idea is to imitate nature,
but on a much smaller scale,
to create mountains and valleys,
rivers and forests,
lakes and fields,
all in a yard
the size of a small room,
where small ponds become lakes,
bushes become trees,
and a block of stone
takes the place of a mountain,
and they even spend a great deal of time
reducing massive trees
down to miniature scale,
with bonsai being a demanding art,
hours spent trimming leaves,
wrapping wire to bend tiny limbs,
roots embedded in rock
and a shallow bed of soil,
daily watering and tending,
all to create a 200-yea-old tree
that is only two-feet tall
but looks just like an ordinary tree
growing in a forest

that no one ever watered
and no one ever trimmed,
which is different,
but also just the same,
as forcing a tree to grow flat on a wall,
trimming away all the limbs
that do not grow in the right direction
or at the desired angle,
trying to correct
something inherently perfect,
which may sound like a fool's errand,
but it is what we do all the time,
not satisfied with the way things are,
unwilling to use and keep things
the way they are,
we try to improve
what reality created over millions of years,
a tree that provides fruit for animals that live there,
animals that protect the tree that provides them with fruit,
a tree that belongs exactly where it is,
an animal that belongs exactly where it is,
and who can design a pond
that will stay the same for a thousand years,
and who can build a temple
that will outlast the mountains,
or who knows how to move
with the grace and coordination
of a school of fish
or a flock of birds
or goats skipping along a mountain cliff?
How much more perfect
can anything be
than a newborn baby's hand,
with tiny nails, and miniature fingers,
so small they hardly seem real?
So as you relax there,
and continue to notice
the changes in your own mind
as you allow yourself
to listen to the things I say
and observe the way your mind

automatically decides
which meaning of each word
is the meaning meant
and which implication of each phrase
is the implication implied,
because there are dear friends
and there are friendly deer,
but there also are deer friends
with antlers on their heads
because they grew them
and not because it is Halloween,
and knowing the difference
is what your brain does
automatically for you,
with no help from you,
and so you can listen to me
with no need to try to make an effort
to try to understand
all the different things
I might be saying to you,
conveying to you
while I seem to be saying one thing,
but am actually saying
something else entirely,
which you really do not need to know
as long as what you hear
is what you need to hear
and all the rest
just goes in one ear
and out the other,
because your brain,
like everything else out there,
is a natural work of art
that is perfectly designed
to do exactly what it does
with no interference or help from you,
and it does it as well as can be done
when you stay out of the way
and stop trying to decide
what a word means or does not mean,
or how to do something

it already knows how to do
much better than you,
and who are you
to tell it differently,
or to think it needs to be
reminded constantly
that it has a job to do,
because you do not know
how to do what it does,
or how to tell a dear from a doe,
or a two from a fro,
which is just one way
that the mind can play
with the way words
can mean so many different things,
like the word run,
which can mean a hundred different things
from running uphill,
to a clock running down
to noses running
and engines running
and people running around
after the home runs in a game,
because what can be more perfect
than a mind that can play
with ideas that way,
and can even measure perfection itself,
so it must be perfect itself,
a perfect measure of perfection
must be perfect itself, must it not?
So let us continue
to give you this opportunity
to relax and enjoy the luxury
of having your eyes closed
and listening to the things I say
without having to make
even the tiniest effort
to try to figure out
what I might say next
or what the words I have already said
might have meant

instead of what you heard,
because it really is ok
to relax and trust your brain
to take care of things here and there,
and everywhere for that matter,
and to ask yourself how it would feel
to actually believe what it tells you
about things around you
being perfect just the way they are,
stunningly harmoniously balanced
no matter what we do,
push in here, it goes out there,
pull out here, it goes in over there,
push up here and it goes down over there,
warm it up here and it cools down over there,
the perfect balance never changes,
it is always there everywhere,
like a teeter totter that shifts and changes
to keep things balanced and level to the ground
no matter who is on either side,
whatever it takes to maintain the balance
always appears, no matter what,
which is why when we try
to make things better
we often end up with a nice big mess,
and when we walk away and leave it alone
it eventually sorts itself out quite nicely,
which probably means
there is a lesson in there somewhere
but chasing after that
would be a waste of time
because it will stay with you
in the background of awareness,
long after you return to wakeful awareness,
and may even still be there with you
as soon as you open your eyes,
so instead just notice your head,
sitting there quietly,
on top of your body
right where it belongs,
full of thoughts, sights, and sounds,

and a gradual feeling of awakening,
of returning to normal wakeful awareness,
and doing so very comfortably,
following a gentle and pleasant path
as effortlessly as a bubble drifts up
in a still quiet pond
and returns to the surface
automatically,
feeling quite refreshed,
rested and aware,
aware of my voice,
aware of taking a deep breath now,
that's right,
aware of waking up
and noticing that the eyes
can be allowed to open now,
that's right,
eyes wide open now,
comfortably awake
and feeling fine,
that's right,
wide awake now.

Chapter 10

Hypnotic Immersions in Universal Love

Tibetan monks reportedly are taught by the Dalai Lama to meditate on "universal compassion for all living beings" as a step
toward personal transformation. In the relevant literature of the
Western world, however, the experience of suddenly loving all life
everywhere is usually described as an outgrowth of a powerful
mystical experience rather than a precipitator of one. We are not
taught that it is a good idea to love everyone. Instead, we are
taught from childhood on to be very careful about whom we talk
to, much less to whom we say, "I love you!" Love is a rare com-
modity to be doled out only to those who deserve it and can be
trusted with it, such as pets, immediate family, and maybe a wor-
thy lover or two. And no matter how often someone says that they
love you, we all tend to believe deep down that this feeling is con-
ditional and subject to revocation at any moment, a suspicion that
is regularly enhanced and supported by a continually growing
divorce rate.

Our cautious attitude belies the fact that loving is an incredibly
easy thing to do as well as an incredibly pleasurable thing to do.
Perhaps our caution is a direct result of just how easy it is. Children
seem to do so without effort or restraint, which may be both a
blessing and a curse. Even though few things feel as good as loving (or have a more profound and beneficial physiological effect),
in our highly mobile society with rising divorce rates, love can be
a dangerous emotional commitment for the young. When a child's
pet fish dies it is a tragedy, when a toy breaks it is a heartbreaking
event, and when a stuffed animal comes apart at the seams it is a
painful loss. But the loss of a friend or a family member in childhood through divorce or moving to another city can be devastating
and can easily lead to the conclusion that it is a very good idea to
be cautious about loving anything or anyone. Some people who
have their hearts broken by the people they love may even learn to

withhold love entirely. This is a primitively effective self-protective measure, even though it also is quite self-defeating. To give up loving in order to avoid the pain is almost as drastic as giving up food to avoid an upset stomach – but many people do it nonetheless. They make a conscious decision to not love anything or anyone ever again.

Loving even one other person necessarily involves the risk of loss, rejection, misunderstanding, and pain. Logically then, loving the entire human race or every living thing would virtually guarantee an ongoing immersion in loss and pain because a great many beings live in horrific conditions, are starving, being injured, falling ill, and dying all the time. Watching such things happen to one person you love would be painful enough. Multiply that by millions or billions and you can understand one side of what it would be like to love the entire human race and every other living thing on earth.

To understand the other side, however, you must first remember the complete joy of loving someone, perhaps for the very first time. Multiply the joyful pleasure and excitement of that feeling by millions and billions and it becomes easier to understand why anyone would be willing to risk the pain of loving all living beings everywhere. Sister Mother Theresa, among others, was fond of pointing out that love and pain go together and that loving others necessarily means resigning oneself to, and even welcoming, the ongoing pain.

Pain is an inherent part of love, just as much a sign and symptom of it as the joy. Thus, to enjoy the immense pleasure of loving all living things, you must be willing to also endure an equal measure of pain. They just go together.

This may sound like a fool's bargain, but remember that pain is simply an indication that something seems out of place, not right, and in need of attention and correction if possible. It is a source of information, nothing more. It may be a source of information that we would just as soon not have, information that we would prefer to ignore, or information that is useless or frustrating because there is nothing that can be done to improve the situation. Nonetheless, it is just information.

It is possible to recognize the nature and source of the suffering of others without entering into that suffering with them. A quiet acceptance of things that cannot be changed, along with a commitment to do whatever can be done to improve the situation, allows loving others to become an immensely joyful and fulfilling experience, perhaps even a significant step toward personal transformation.

It is worth noting that for the Tibetan monks there is no implied promise of being loved by others in return. What is prescribed by the Dalai Lama is the joy of loving others, of a loving compassion for all living things. This is an externally directed emotion, an opening of the heart outward toward everyone and everything, with no thought toward being loved in return. It is an unselfish giving of one's Self.

But the scripts presented in this chapter also recognize that this loving feeling tends to go full circle, perhaps eventually revealing a quiet love of Self, and, more importantly, an overwhelmingly powerful sensation of love and support from all life on earth and even from the seemingly unfeeling universe itself. The other forms of life on earth nurture us by providing us with the food and oxygen we need to survive. What a loving thing to do. And ultimately, it is the dynamic energies of a seemingly cold and uncaring universe that create life itself and provide the environmental forces that define and sustain each of us. What a loving thing to do.

You are a part of the universe and it is a part of you. You were created from and by it and it, in turn, deserves to be recognized and appreciated by you. This seems to be a legitimate basis for a mutually loving relationship, or at least for the perception of a mutually interdependent relationship. Some people may be more comfortable attributing the creative forces of the universe to a particular god or a supernatural being and if that is the case for you, so be it. If it is easier for you to feel love for and from a god than from an infinite universe, then that is fine with me. Either way, we end up with a transformational connection to everyone and everything around us. By loving and being loved, we end up getting exactly what we need. As others have already pointed out, all we need is love.

Creation
In the beginning
there was the word,
and the words spoken
in the beginning
of a trance state of mind
are just some words spoken
to help things move along
just as I am speaking to you now,
and so if you close your eyes now
you can listen to those words
more comfortably and
begin to relax more fully,
because it does not matter
what I say,
you can hear
whatever words you need to hear,
because even though many people believe
that there are special words
that must be spoken,
"special words" that need to be said
in special ways
to create all the different parts
of a deep hypnotic trance,
words that can pull you into a trance
whether you want to go
or not go right now,
when all along, of course
there are no such words
that have that kind of power,
because it all belongs to you
all of the power over you
and your own thoughts
belongs to you
and the only thing that words can do
is help you wonder
what you yourself can do
to discover how easy it can be
to simply let go now
and begin to allow yourself to drift
into a light trance,

or a medium trance
but not yet a deep, deep trance,
even though
you may be ready to go
much more deeply down
than before,
and that is fine,
just take your own sweet time
to do things in your own way
and in your own time
because some words
are more useful
than others
at reminding the mind
of things known and not known before,
things felt and not felt before,
because the power of any word
to create anything
does not come from that word,
the power to create
comes from reminding the mind
about something you have heard,
or something you saw,
or something you felt
and know about now,
about how something is,
but some words
do not need to be heard,
do not need to be spoken
to be the beginning
of a deep comfortable trance
or the start of a quiet realization
that the heart already knows
all it needs to know.
From the very beginning
you knew how
to understand fairy tales
about kisses breaking spells,
and the search for glass slippers,
of lost loves,
because before you learned to read

you already knew how to love,
you already held things
in a quiet embrace,
loved colors with your eyes,
knew animals in books,
felt protected and loved
by something you carried around
and you even loved figments
of other people's imagination,
imaginary characters in imaginary places,
and not so very long ago
you first felt yourself loved,
totally loved,
adored and respected,
admired and revered,
enjoyed and appreciated
for doing nothing at all,
except being you,
which may have been
a surprise at the time,
something unexpected
and even difficult
to really believe,
but because it was so long ago
you opened your heart
without even trying,
not holding anything back,
just loving completely,
which some people say
is just biochemistry at work,
the right hormones
and the right neurotransmitters
in the right parts of the brain
to make mothers care
about their babies,
and to make people snuggle together
so that the species will survive,
but children everywhere
carry stuffed animals everywhere,
they cling to them,
and miss them,

and care about them deeply,
they love those stuffed animals,
perhaps more than most people
love each other,
or even themselves,
and what does that say
about your ability
to love something,
just because you do,
not because you have to,
but just because you do,
and so I wonder
if you can remember
that you do have that ability
to love anything at all,
to love a smell,
to love the sunlight,
the warmth on your skin,
to love the softness of dusty earth,
and the smoothness of it too,
to love a picture in a book,
to cut it out to save it for later on,
and to care deeply
about a nest of baby birds,
to embrace it all,
the wonder of it all,
the joy of it all,
the happiness of rolling down a hill,
the thrill of splashing in a puddle,
the pleasure of a best friend at school,
easily and automatically caring,
a child loves without restraint,
a child loves without trying,
and so sitting there
in a trance state of mind,
quietly aware
that you were once a child
who could love without trying
you already know and realize
that it is not that easy any more
to open that door,

to embrace all life with love
to feel love all the time,
it is not that easy any more
to even know where to go
to find that feeling,
or to give yourself permission
to care about anything that way,
but that possibility
is still very real for you,
and the memory of doing it
is still very real for you,
and all you need to do
to find it within you
is to remember that place
where it can slip on through
back into awareness for a change,
which only requires
a little imagination
to test out different possibilities,
to see what reconnects your awareness
to that feeling deep inside,
where all you need to do
is to just pay attention
to see what opens that door,
to find that key
that allows you to begin
loving things fully again,
or to just begin remembering
how it felt back then,
automatically reconnecting
even though it is always hard to know,
at first,
where those keys might be,
where that door is located,
and so I would like you
to have an opportunity
to try out different things
to see what works for you,
because I really do not know
what words or ideas might work for you,
I do not know, for example,

if holding a warm purring kitten
would touch your heart,
or perhaps the thought
of a playful puppy
or a chirping chick
is more up your alley,
or would a bluebird on your shoulder
bring a bigger smile,
and all the while just one question
that you need to ask yourself and answer,
of all the things that you could hold,
of all the things you have embraced,
which one touches your heart more
when you think about it,
which one brings the biggest tears of joy
to your smiling face,
and how many different people, places, things
are you lucky enough
to have to sort through
across time and space
to find your way down into
the center of that place,
the purest core of that love
for all creatures great and small,
for all trees and flowers too,
for seashells and sparkly rocks
and all the other things
that children everywhere love,
because the world is a magical mystery tour
and it all belongs to you,
so that you can allow yourself the luxury
of embracing it all with your mind,
holding it all close to you now
and recognizing how it feels
to be a part of it all,
and to have it all be a part of you,
as if you are it all
and you can touch it all
at the same time,
every wave on the ocean,
every breath of wind,

every fish and bird,
every leaf and flower,
every animal,
every child,
every human being
who ever was, is, or shall be,
all connected to you,
all embraced by you,
all a part of you,
and the amazing part is
that you actually do have the capacity
to love it all in the same way
that it all loves you,
completely and without hesitation,
even though you already know
that love is just another word
for nothing left to lose,
and in the beginning
there was just a word,
a word that began this process
of drifting into a light trance
or a deep trance
and wondering how it feels
to feel those things quite deeply
and at the same time
to feel them begin to drift away
as the mind begins to return
to normal wakeful awareness now,
with seeds sown,
and doors opened,
and the cat out of the bag,
so you might as well relax
and let those understandings
drift back upwards with you
and snuggle in beside you
as you return to wakeful awareness now,
able to be aware quite comfortably
that the mind can awaken quite automatically
and eyes can be allowed to open again
while wakeful awareness returns
more and more completely,

and you return feeling rested and refreshed,
very comfortable,
not really sure,
perhaps,
what that was all about,
and that is fine,
because they were just words
that reminded you
of some things that you already knew
that still belong to you
even as you drift upwards
quite completely now,
eyes open,
and wide awake,
that's right.

Countdown

Let's begin today
with a countdown,
a numerical way
to launch you
into a deeper trance
of comfortable relaxation
than you may have been before,
where you can find it easier and easier
to listen to the things I might say,
while you take your own time
to find a way to enjoy
allowing the mind to wander
to those places we can talk about
later on,
but in the meantime
beginning that countdown,
the way NASA does
before blasting off for space,
with ten
and then nine
and then eight,
and with each count
feeling yourself letting go a bit more,
getting ready to begin to explore

those places in you
where you can be aware of things
that otherwise
might go overlooked,
but become quite apparent to you
later on,
as you enter into
that effortless state
of relaxed awareness,
where the countdown continues now
to seven,
and you drift down a bit more,
and then down to six,
where things begin to seem
a bit easier and easier,
even though the anticipation continues
with five,
but you are halfway there,
and then four,
counting down,
working toward an end,
moving toward something desired
like the steps involved
in falling in love,
which can be done slowly,
step by step,
one step at a time
in a cautious way,
not moving too fast,
just taking time to be sure
that each step is safe and secure,
that it really is ok
to feel that way
about someone else
that you have just begun to get to know,
although others may do it differently,
falling for another
all at once,
jumping right into it
fully and completely,
going for it all at first glance,

wanting to make one and one
become two,
and make that two become three
before you know it,
because counting down
from four to three
can be done quickly,
before you know it,
but it also can be done slowly,
one step at a time,
carefully and deeply,
moving very slowly down
from four to three,
taking your own time
before counting down to two,
because two and two are four,
but before going on any more
we need to explore the idea
that two can be too much
for anyone to hold onto,
or it can seem like a perfect balance,
something easy to do,
the way you have two arms
and two feet,
two ears and two eyes,
two legs and two hands
to hold onto things with,
to embrace those you love
carefully or quickly,
feeling the warmth of holding someone,
as the countdown continues
from two down to one
and that one could be someone
you love more than you know,
because you do not yet know
who that someone is,
because you have not yet met them
and yet you can love them
more than you know,
just as deeply and completely
as anyone you do know,

just as fully and completely,
with all your heart and soul,
and you can know now
how it feels to do so,
how it feels to love them that way
even though you do not even know
who that person is
because we are not there yet,
we are still counting down to one,
down to that one someone you love
who also is everyone you do not know,
but could know sometime,
and everyone you already know at the same time,
someone who loves you even more
than you might imagine someone could,
someone who does not yet exist
except in your own mind,
hidden in that quiet place
deep down inside,
not just one person
but everyone you could ever know,
everything that ever is,
as the count down continues
down on to one
and then blastoff comes next,
and someone throws a switch
that releases the latch
and lets things take off,
and launches that feeling
off into space,
a feeling of deep quiet love
breaking free and taking off,
a passionate and noisy power,
breaking free of gravity
and floating up and away,
a deep and happy feeling,
perhaps deeper and freer
than any you have ever known,
because you can love someone
not known
and even something not knowable

with passion and power
unrestrained in any way
as a way to discover
how much there is there
in that ability to love
that is difficult to share,
absolute and complete
and totally connected,
revealing a feeling
from a long time ago,
from childhood perhaps,
or even before,
a moment perhaps
when that door opened wide
and you loved something fully,
more than anything ever,
it just seemed quite perfect
and perfectly wonderful,
a gift of wonder and delight,
able to enjoy the beauty
and the perfection
and to feel the connection,
able to give your heart away
completely,
able to enjoy that moment of that day
completely,
able right now,
while drifting deep in space,
relaxed and yet aware of listening
to your own thoughts and feelings,
able now to imagine being aware
of how it feels to feel that way,
how it feels to love that way,
how it would feel to love everything
that way,
to care about everyone that way,
to care about every living thing that way,
to look at every face that way,
to see every bird and beast that way,
to smile at every baby that way,
to caress every flower that way,

to feel the wonder of holding something alive,
to be stunned by a crystal,
amazed by a rainbow,
awed by the universe,
because you do have the ability
to appreciate the miracle
of life itself,
of the existence of things,
even a rock,
and you have the capacity
to love such things
more deeply than you might imagine,
more completely than you may believe,
a feeling of loving compassion
an ability to enjoy the joy
of being a part
of all there is everywhere,
connected to it all,
to the life force of it all,
to the energy within,
the energy of life within you,
the energy of suns and stars
the energy of it all as far as you can see,
an energy that you can feel too,
as you turn your attention toward it,
toward that spark of life,
that fire of energy
deep down within,
that blazing fire of creation
burning within you,
and all around you as well,
an energy that seems to grow
as you pay attention to it,
becoming brighter and more powerful,
unbearably bright at times,
and soothingly intense as well,
a world aglow
in the fires of life,
blazing and lighting the way
in the search for you
before you became you,

that inner light,
that original life
that was there long before
you even knew you were a you
and is out there everywhere
and will be there long after you are there,
because even as you relax here today,
and drift down into you that way,
the rest of you
is out there everywhere
connected to everything,
a part of everything,
drifting is space and time,
filling up space and time,
experiencing the universe,
a universe of experiences,
while your conscious mind
drifts back down here,
gliding back to the ground,
back where you started
back before the countdown began,
back to the beginning of it all
where you can begin to return
to normal wakeful awareness now,
that's right,
gradually or rapidly returning
with a feeling of rested wakefulness
and a recognition
that you do not need to try
to bother making
all the effort it would take
to remember all those things
you were thinking
or all those things
that were said to you,
because you can drift back
the way you drift back from dreams,
remembering some things
and forgetting others for a time,
with the full assurance
that your unconscious mind

can decide what to keep
and what to save for later on,
even as you continue to drift upwards
and take a deep breath now,
and let it out,
that's right,
returning to wakefulness more and more,
comfortably drifting back
and aware of the chair,
aware of arms and legs,
aware of becoming more and more aware,
and of allowing the eyes to open now,
that's right,
eyes open
and wakeful awareness returns now
quite completely!

An Embrace
As you close your eyes now,
and begin to relax
a bit more than before,
but not as much yet
as you can later on,
you can continue to listen
to the things that I say
because this business of a trance,
drifting into a trance,
can at first seem quite difficult
or confusing
even though
there really is nothing
that you need to do at all
except continue to allow yourself
to listen to the things I say
and to allow your mind
to drift into a trance
in your own time
and in your own way,
a light trance,
or a deep trance,
whatever occurs along the way

is just fine,
that's right,
because no one really knows
how much more deeply relaxed
you might be able to become,
and you do not need to know
exactly how or when
you drift into that trance
where things happen automatically,
the way the mind drifts
automatically
down toward that place
deep down inside,
the center of the center
of a quiet effortless space,
a place of calm contentment
and pleasant drifting thoughts,
the way a pebble drifts automatically
down toward the center of things
in that quiet pool in the mind,
into that silent place deep down inside,
a place of relaxed awareness,
a place where it is safe to hide,
a place where you know how it feels
to feel things for real,
to be really aware of things intensely
for a change,
to embrace those feelings easily
and to feel ok knowing
that you already know
how it feels to let go,
and to hold that feeling close to you,
to hold it in your arms,
feeling the warmth of caring,
enjoying the peace of sharing
that soft gentle feeling
that begins deep down inside,
holding it gently in your hands,
in your arms,
in your effortless embrace
in that safe secure place

where it really is ok
to feel ok for a while
about allowing the mind
to reach out that way,
to pay close attention for a while
to a person you really love
to someone you really enjoy,
to someone you care about
more deeply than you ever thought you could
perhaps,
but not as much as you actually could
perhaps,
and that's fine,
because continuing to relax
and drifting on down
you can begin to discover
how many other people
share that quiet space with you
because you invite them in
and hold them softly in your heart,
the way a small child
loves a playful puppy,
the way you might love
that small child,
or someone else perhaps
even more than you allowed yourself before,
because you can allow yourself
to care about them that way,
in that deeply caring way
that ordinarily we restrain or hide,
even though it is so easy
to remember feeling that feeling
many times before,
a sudden surge of feeling
for a person
or even an animal,
embracing it in the mind,
caressing it,
caring and smiling at the same time,
overcome with emotion they say,
and yet it is so easy to do,

to feel that feeling in the eyes,
to feel that smile in the face,
to feel that tightness in the throat,
to feel that melting of the heart
that looks out at it all,
and envelopes it all,
all the creatures large and small,
all the people short and tall,
all a part of the same thing,
all connected each to all,
to put your arms around it all
for just a moment or two
that's all,
letting it all out
for a brief time,
that surge of caring
for a brief time,
remembering how it was
as a child
to love more than ever since,
and knowing ever since
how easy it will be later on
to allow yourself to love,
with a mother's love,
a father's love,
a sister's love,
or a brother's love,
each for the other,
loving one another
forever and ever,
but you know quite well
that I can talk about it,
now and forever,
and nothing will really happen
until you open that door
and allow the mind to explore
that place it has been to before,
a place deep within,
a quiet comfortable place,
full of soft intensity
and a smiling lightness of being,

as if floating upwards
on a warm cloud,
or a balloon filled
with laughing gas
that fills the mind
with thoughts of puppies
chasing butterflies,
or childhood dreams
of rolling downhill
in the cool wet grass
and sifting soft dust through fingers
on a warm summer day,
but so much more than that
becomes available
with each step down,
with each letting go and drifting down
you can move down even closer
than you have ever been before
to that particular place deep inside
that loves it all at once,
all of everything at the same time,
a place where you can feel
that feeling of holding them all
in a softly smiling embrace,
holding them all in your arms,
all those children
and puppies
and kittens everywhere,
small and tall,
young and old,
here and there,
and all those creatures too
from the tiniest fish,
no bigger than a gnat,
to the whales that fly
though water
and the hawks that soar
through air,
because you can soar there too,
or climb the rock red cliffs
the way those lions do,

and search for berries in the brush
or dig up mushrooms in the woods,
and scamper sideways like a crab
along a rocky shore,
and so much more,
because it all
belongs to you,
and it all is right there,
deep within you,
like diving down
beneath the surface
to see the clouds of living color
on the coral reefs around the world,
more life down there
than anyone can see from the surface,
just like you are too,
are you not?
So full of life down there inside,
able to see and feel it all,
to hold it all inside the mind
to embrace it all as one,
one living earth,
a living breathing thing,
to hold it all right there,
in the palm of your hand,
in the center of your mind
and it really is ok
to be surprised to realize
that you really can
love it all,
as if it were
a newborn child,
a fragile infant
full of life
and full of promise,
and you may love it for what it is,
that soft and living earth,
but also all the different things
it might become later on,
as it grows and changes
and changes and grows,

and each part comes and goes,
becoming something new
while continuing something old,
just as some things continue within you
as you begin to drift back now,
without letting go
of a tender feeling
that can be difficult to find at first,
but gets easier and easier over time,
just as it gets easier and easier
for the mind to drift upwards now
back toward the surface
of wakeful awareness
where you can take a deep breath now
and feel wakeful awareness returning
quite comfortably,
as the body awakens
and the mind continues
to hold on comfortably
to all there is,
even as it drifts upwards now as well,
and gradually returns
to the surface of awareness now,
where the eyes can be allowed to open
and wakeful awareness return,
that's right,
wide awake now,
where you can tell me,
as you allow your eyes to open
and a pleasant wakeful alertness
to continue,
you can tell me now,
"How are you feeling,
right now?"

Chapter 11

Hypnotic Oneness with the Cosmos

As noted in Chapter 1, the loss of a sense of Self is the most frequently proposed explanation in the psychological and consciousness literature of the onset of a cosmic consciousness episode. Thus, when I first began trying to use hypnosis to create mystical states, I believed that mere entry into an undifferentiated, egoless, or empty state of mind, such as that obtained while in a meditative trance, is a necessary and sufficient precondition for the spontaneous emergence of a spiritual or cosmic event. Unfortunately, as I discussed above, it is not that simple.

We all lose our sense of Self for brief moments here and there all the time without even noticing it, much less becoming immersed in a mystical state because of it. Most of the time we remember to stay oriented for person, place, and time, but every now and then we lose ourselves entirely in a book, a movie, a thought, or just staring off into space and we forget to pay attention to who, where, or when we are for a while. Then we snap out of it, reorient, and get on with our life. The same could be said of an hypnotic trance. It is an incredibly comfortable state of passively absorbed attention during which the conscious definition of ordinary reality, including the Self, is allowed to become flexible or even evaporate for a time. But such a state is not automatically mystical. Eventually, after floating around aimlessly in empty space or drifting in captivating fantasies for a while, we snap out of it and go on about our business.

Becoming a blank slate devoid of personal memory or identity may provide an opportunity for mystical states, but it is not a trigger event in and of itself. Entering into either a meditative trance or a hypnotic trance is not sufficient, by itself, to create a peak or transformational experience. Something extraordinary is required to move the passive quietness of a trance state into an explosive experience of dramatic change. Contrary to my original emphasis on the destruction of the Self as the essential ingredient for the attainment of cosmic consciousness, therefore, I now maintain that mystical or cosmic consciousness does not occur until or unless the quietness of an egoless trance is replaced by an explosive flash of thoughts, sensations, and/or emotions that ultimately center around and produce an intense awareness of beauty, truth, perfection, and the connection of everything to everything else and, ultimately, the perfectly beautiful oneness of the cosmos.

Now, I feel like it must be said at this point that the universe you experience is only as beautiful or ugly as you think it is. The universe itself (and everything in it) is neither beautiful nor ugly – it just is. Beauty is something the human mind imposes, as is perfection or any other judgmental quality. Thus, even though it may be conceptually useful to talk about experiencing "the perfectly beautiful oneness of the cosmos", what is really involved is much more straightforward. "Awe", that is the essence of the experience. Stunned, amazed, astounded, and overwhelmed, just plain AWE. That is the simplest way to convey the effect of a direct awareness of the divine miracle of everything.

There are many possible pathways to that outcome. The previous chapters offer a variety of opportunities to slip in through one side door or another. By concentrating on one relatively minor component of the overall experience, such as a bright light, a chorus of sound, a pleasant physical sensation, or a joyful emotion, these approaches begin on the periphery and then gradually move toward a central climactic merging with the creative forces of the universe. These approaches represent an indirect approach which may or may not ever get to that climactic cosmic connection of becoming one with and awestruck by the oneness of everything.

The route provided in the current chapter, on the other hand, involves a direct entry through the front door and straight down into the main hall. There is no step by step build up to the core experience, no dipping your toes into the shallow end to get used to the sensation. The scripts presented in this chapter each involve a relatively rapid all-or-nothing plunge toward the center of things. They promote a direct immersion in and identification with the power, harmony, wisdom, and benevolence of the cosmos.

Although this procedure may be the fastest and most efficient way to get there, it is not necessarily the best route for most people to take. It is a bit like throwing someone into the deep end of an Olympic size pool to see if they can figure out how to swim. That might be worth a try but only if the person already knows how to float. Ideally, therefore, the direct plunges toward the center of the action presented in this chapter will be reserved for those who have dabbled in the shallow end of the pool for a while and discovered how to float and how to move fairly comfortably through minor altered states and mystical mists.

As always, if an approach seems to be too much too fast or if it fails to move awareness in the desired direction, just stop and use a different, more comfortable entryway instead. There is no exactly right way to do this after all. Whatever works for someone is the right way for them, but not necessarily for anyone else. It may take a lot of false starts to locate a strategy that works for any given individual. So use what works and scrap the rest.

Cosmic Connections

As you begin to relax now
and allow your mind to drift,
I want you to know
that a hypnotic trance
is really nothing special,
it is just a state of relaxed attention,
a quiet state of mind
where things happen automatically,
the same way your foot sometimes
automatically steps on the brake
when you are in the back seat of a car,
or the way you can reach out
and catch a ball
without even thinking about it,
or the way your mind
automatically understands
the meaning of my words,
even when those words
can have many different meanings,
so that the mind understands
that a deer can be beautiful

but what is beautiful to you
can be dear to you too,
and things can seem to mean one thing
but turn out to mean something else entirely
because it all belongs to you
even as you enter into a light trance
or a medium trance
or a really deep trance now,
where it is quite ok
to relax in every way
and allow the mind to drift down that way,
in the same effortless way
that a pebble drifts down
in a quiet still pond
and comes to rest on the bottom,
the same quiet way that you
can continue now
to drift on down
while you listen to the sound of my voice
and automatically understand
the particular meaning of the things I say
and the particular way
that they allow you to do
what you need to do
to enter into a trance now
and to pay close attention now
as I begin to explain
what we are going to do here today,
what you can do here today,
if it is ok with you,
to begin to explore,
even more than before perhaps,
the way things are connected
one to another,
like Tinker Toys or Legos,
everything superglued together,
the way atoms stick together
and the way you are stuck
to everything that is connected
to everything everywhere,
but before we can even begin

to examine the way things are put together,
you probably already know
that the very first thing to do
is to take them all apart,
the way a child takes things apart
to see how they work,
clocks and CD players and toys that move,
they all come apart at the seams
to be examined carefully,
but I do not know
if you already know
how much fun it is
when the pieces of those things
all fit back together again,
just the way they used to,
everything in its place
connected all together,
which is very different
from having pieces scattered all around
that do nothing at all by themselves
and only work when all connected together
in just the right ways,
like jigsaw puzzle pieces
all connected together
to reveal the whole picture
with nothing missing or misplaced,
or Sudoku puzzles
that only work right
when just the right numbers
are in exactly the right place
in each row and each column,
a perfectly placed pattern of different things,
which is different from
a perfectly placed pattern of similar things,
like rows of bricks in a wall
or tiles one after another on a floor,
but then there is a checkerboard pattern too,
and woven patterns in weavings,
that can be simple or complex
like the weavings in blankets and carpets
from all over the world,

woven by hand
on simple looms,
with different colors of thread
dyed with roots and leaves,
creating gorgeous patterns,
each meaning something special
to the people who wove them,
the way the Navaho wove rugs
with patterns of plants and people
but always remembered
to leave a knot, an imperfection,
to not compete with the creator
of all that is everywhere
who created the only perfect thing
that there is anywhere,
and that thing is this place here
and there and everywhere
and everything in that place,
which, as you know,
of course includes you,
because you are a part of it all too,
just like the sun, the stars,
and everything in between,
all that starlight flying around
filling up the universe
at the speed of light,
which is what we are doing here today,
connecting it all together
and filling up your mind
with thoughts that move
at the speed of light,
following those grooves in thought,
the way a wheel follows the ruts in a dirt road,
or water follows the grooves we call rivers
that lead from one place to another,
from one thought to another,
never stopping to wonder
why to flow in that direction
and to make that connection,
because that is just the way thoughts go
from one place to another,

one thought to another,
slowly coming to an end
where they all flow together
like the sea,
the sea of love,
a sea of loving thoughts
a sea of thoughts about love
and thoughts about everything else as well,
all thoughts flowing together there,
melting into each other there,
in your mind
becoming part of each other there,
and wondering what happens
when thoughts begin to evaporate
and rise up into thin air and blow away
and become clouds drifting past
in different shapes and sizes
that have no real form or meaning
but can look like anything
the mind can imagine,
like Donald Duck and Goofy perhaps,
or whales with large hats,
a boat with bat wings,
or a man with a large nose
that grows over time
and becomes longer and longer
right before your eyes,
while particles of thought
continue to separate,
to stretch out thinner and thinner,
until the mind finally becomes clear
with the bright blue sky
of a summer's day,
and then your body slowly dissolves
into particles of sensation,
the way sugar dissolves
in warm soothing water,
each piece letting go of the others,
spreading out to fill the space,
staying in touch somehow
while also floating up and away,

and becoming a cloud of sensations
that blow around with the breeze
and seep out into the wind,
escaping from here to there,
traveling everywhere,
particles of you in the air,
moving away faster and faster,
flying off in all directions,
blasting off into space,
out to the sun
blasting us with light and energy,
all those photons and protons,
electrons and neutrinos,
coming at us,
going through us,
and you going up at it,
and all of it going off toward the stars
swirling energies of life,
swirling energies of the universe,
swirling particles all the same age,
all going back to the beginning,
the beginning of everything,
the creation of every particle,
tiny packages of energy
that became sunlight,
starlight,
moonlight,
and by the light of a fire
became the earth,
a place full of particles,
some of which became you
while others became others,
and so the question is,
how far out can you feel,
out beyond you
out into the room,
out into the air
and out onto the sun
out to the stars
out into the past
where it all began,

where the particles of you
began as something new,
something never seen before,
and grew and grew
into everything
all around,
and into you too,
a drop in the sea,
a part of all there is everywhere,
a speck of sand
on a never ending beach,
able to be aware
that there are more connections
between cells in your brain
than there are grains of sand
on all the beaches of the world
or stars in the universe,
more thoughts than atoms in everything,
including the thought
that you are where the universe
begins to become aware
of itself,
and you are the universe
being aware of itself,
you are the awareness
of the universe itself,
different patterns of different particles
arranged in different ways
that allow you to see, to hear, to feel
and to understand things,
all connected together,
those thoughts, feelings, sounds and sights
all connected together
within you,
like that bright point of light
when a magnifying glass
focuses sunlight
on that one tiny spot,
a tiny spot in you
where it all comes together
and the mind sees it all

219

at the same time,
feels it all
at the same time,
hears it all
at the same time,
out to the edges of the universe,
a symphony of energies
pulsating in every galaxy, star, and sun,
in the spaces between thoughts,
the fullness of space
from the beginning of time
that fills the mind
and comes together right there
with an understanding of all that is,
with an awareness of touching it all,
an awareness of it all touching you,
coming together there
deep within you,
and you deep within it,
becoming it now,
moving with it now,
and it moving with you,
it becoming you,
and you becoming it,
flowing together in a rush of sensation,
moving faster and smoother than before,
deeper and deeper into that space,
going backwards in space and time
to another time a long time ago
before words,
just sensations then,
sensations you could taste and smell,
sensations that go on and on,
and become all there is for a time,
with you allowing it all
to absorb you,
to become you,
to transport you
higher and higher,
farther and farther away,
right to edge of it all,

hanging on and holding back,
but getting closer and closer,
being pulled over that edge,
sliding right over that edge,
and then a letting go,
a release of all that effort
and a plunging off into
the emptiness of space,
flowing right on through
to the other side someplace
letting go of it all now
and knowing it all now,
even as you begin now
to become you once again,
breathing in and breathing out,
with all of your thoughts,
and all of your sensations,
all of your energies,
and all of your molecules and atoms
coming back together again,
putting you back together again,
arms and legs reconnected to you,
all the parts of you back to you,
separating you from the rest of it all,
the way a finger
is separated
from the toes and the legs
and all the other parts
that it can touch
even though it is
still a part of it all,
and all of it is a part of you
and you a part of it,
being here now,
perhaps even more than before,
being aware of some things
more than others
and able to become more aware
later on,
and that's fine,
because for now

all you need to do
is to allow the mind
to drift back into awareness,
a wakeful awareness
where all those things
you were thinking about before
can drift into the background,
like a dream,
even though some things
can drift back up with you,
back to the surface of awareness now,
and other things can stay back there
for use later on when needed,
and that is fine,
because you can enjoy
some thoughts and understandings now
about some parts of this experience
that can be quite useful,
and allow the rest to rest for now
as you return to normal wakeful awareness,
rested and refreshed,
and becoming comfortably awake and alert now,
aware of where you are,
aware of the room,
of arms and legs,
of your eyes beginning to open,
that's right,
and you can become aware
that your eyes
can be allowed to be open now,
that's right,
as you return to wakeful awareness
quite completely.
That's right,
wide awake now!

Unifications

Resting there now
I want you to make sure
that you are comfortable,
very comfortable in all respects,

before we begin,
because what you are going to do
requires you to be comfortable enough
to pay close attention
to everything I say
and to also pay close attention
to everything that happens to you
along the way,
which can be a pretty tall order
unless we simplify matters first,
so let's begin by pointing out
that you have a left leg and a right leg
and you do not really have to try
to make an effort
to pay close attention to them at all
for a time,
they can each take care of themselves just fine
while you pay attention to other things,
because you also have a right arm and a right hand
and a left arm and a left hand
and you do not really have to try
to make an effort
to pay close attention to them at all either,
because they can also take care of themselves just fine
while you pay attention to other things
and allow yourself to relax
and listen to the things I say,
as well as your own thoughts and sensations,
while your head rests there on your shoulders
without any help from you
or any need for you to pay attention to it,
and so it is like hanging things up,
different parts of you
that you will not need for a while,
like hanging up coats and hats,
taking off boots and gloves,
and knowing they will still be there
when you want to put them back on,
but in the meantime
it really is ok
to put them away somewhere

where there is no need
to pay attention to them,
so it is ok
to allow the mind to take them all off,
all those parts of you,
to disconnect itself from arms and legs,
to forget about the head for a time,
but then you also have a front and a back,
do you not,
and even an inside and an outside,
and you do not need to bother
making an effort
to pay close attention to those things
for a time either,
you can feel
what you need to feel,
where you need to feel it,
without having to make an effort
to put your finger on it,
or to grasp it in any way,
because even as you slip into a trance
the mind can slide
to where it needs to be
without any effort from you
where it can be in touch with things
that are difficult to hold on to,
and it is just so much easier
to allow things to happen by themselves
over time,
to enter awareness in their own way
over time,
to move into the mind in their own time,
and in their own way,
with no effort at all,
and all you have to do
is nothing at all,
just opening your mind
and allowing things through
into the center of you,
down to that part of you
that the mind returns to now,

though it may take you a while
to really allow things
to go all the way there,
and that is fine for now,
because in dreams we can walk
and we can talk,
we can hear things and see things,
we can touch things and be touched,
without trying to do
anything at all,
because the mind does it all for us,
even things
we do not expect it to do,
because it is also true
that some things
just happen on their own,
like magic,
making something out of nothing,
the ways seeds grow into trees
or turtles grow a shell
or caterpillars dissolve
and rearrange their cells
to make butterflies
that flap their wings and flutter
from one place to another
without looking like they know
where they are going to go,
but they always seem to manage
to get where they need to be
without going there directly,
going up and down and around instead
and eventually landing on that flower,
that one kind of flower
made just for it
where it can fit
and suck up the nectar
while the flower gives it pollen
to carry to the next,
a different way of doing things
of making new things,
with each providing something

to the other along the way,
but that is not surprising
is it,
because everywhere it is the same
where all life seems to enjoy
doing those things
that make more life,
and all life seems to enjoy the possibility
of doing things in just the right way
to make more of itself,
which makes me wonder
about matter itself,
the basis of all life,
and how it feels
about making more of itself
and what does it feel like
for one particle
to be attracted to another,
to be drawn together
and to merge together,
and to become something new,
a new molecule,
releasing energy along the way,
connecting together
and releasing huge amounts of energy,
pulsating surges of energy
like that of the sun,
like that of every star,
millions and billions of them,
each a sphere of nuclear reactions,
a primordial mass of powerful forces,
a ball of particles touching and connecting,
contracting down while surging up
to a huge release of white hot intensity,
moving and flowing around and around,
erupting at times in flares of fire,
continuous rushes of light and heat,
white hot heat,
like the heat of passion
an unending supply of intensity
compressed down,

right in the center of it all,
the origin of it all,
the source of it all,
and what a sound that must be,
how incredibly unbearably bright it must be,
how overwhelmingly intense it must feel,
all that power,
a trillion H-bombs
all at once
in one place
at one time
forever and ever,
a never ending explosion
that is the ongoing creation
of all that is,
just imagine that,
just for an instant,
how it feels to release
all that pent up energy
all at once,
with an enormous intensity
that never stops,
that just keeps going and going,
unimaginably, unbelievably, unendingly,
on and on and on,
everywhere,
sending out torrents of energy
that become clouds of particles
that become everything,
droplets of energy
condensing into plants,
breathing life into animals,
creating rain,
powering each thought
in each brain,
sparking ideas,
illuminating understandings,
providing everything needed
for things to be
just the way they are,
and for you to be

just the way you are,
a product of that star,
stardust pulled together
for a brief time
in this particular form
that is you,
and later on
more stardust pulled together
to keep you happy and fed and warm too,
so right now,
each particle of you
used to be a part of something else too,
and all these particles
from different places,
pieces of many different things,
all got pulled together in you,
all held together like glue,
at least for now,
losing some at times,
adding new ones at times,
all of them borrowed for a time
like books from a library,
energy on loan,
that's you,
and that is everyone else too,
some parts long overdue
others brand new,
all of them connected together,
all of them pieces of that sun,
particles of energy
born in the fires of the universe,
trapped for a time in your mind,
but where were you
before you knew you were you,
and when did you stop
remembering that you are
a part of it all,
and how does it feel
to let go and to know
that all of it is you,
and you are all of it too,

the way each blood cell
that flows through you,
and goes one way or another,
and does what it is supposed to do,
does what is was made to do,
is a part of you,
is a piece of what you are,
that is the way that you
are a part of the universe
that goes one way or another
and does what you were made to do,
to walk and run and see and feel,
to be that part
that does those things
for the universe,
the way those blood cells
do things in you for you,
because it is difficult to remember
that the energy of the sun
is what runs it all
and that energy
is the energy you feel
whenever you feel
anything at all,
the energy you see,
the energy you hear,
the energy you taste and smell,
it is the energy of it all,
including all thoughts,
and even the awareness
that you are sitting there
listening to me
is a part of that energy,
the same energy you feel
when you begin to drift
back toward the surface of awareness,
back to the sound of this room,
back into a recognition
that some things
are already fading away,
while others seem to stand out

and return to wakeful awareness
with you,
as you return now
step by step
back to normal wakeful awareness
where the eyes can be allowed to open
and wakeful awareness
can return quite comfortably
and quite completely now,
that's right,
eyes open now
and wide awake.

Magnifications
Let's begin today
by giving you
all the opportunity you need
to move into a comfortable trance state,
a deep hypnotic state
where you can listen to the things I say
and give yourself permission
to simply allow events to happen,
and to allow yourself the luxury
of using your own unconscious mind
to experience exactly what you need,
but maybe not exactly
what you think you are looking for,
something that otherwise
might be very difficult
or confusing,
even though it might also be fun,
the same way it might be fun
to suddenly be Superman,
or to have super powers for a while,
or even to just have three wishes
from that genie in a bottle,
or to be able to fly,
or to be in charge of everything
and able to control it all,
things that are difficult
to imagine being

and that means
that you need to be able
to be comfortably relaxed
and effortlessly aware
of all the different things
I will be saying to you
later on,
because becoming like a god
or having newfound powers
is exactly what this is all about today,
and so you need to take some time now,
all the time you need,
to drift into a really good trance for a while,
a light trance,
or a medium trance
or a nice deep trance for a change,
a trance where you can allow things
to change inside and out
and continue to be comfortable
just being relaxed and aware
of all those things occurring along the way,
so you can take your own time
to create that trance state of mind,
which is much easier than you might think,
because all you need to be able to do
to enter into that trance
is nothing at all for awhile,
which is easy to say,
but finding your own way
to relax that way
and to just allow things to occur
in their own way
while you do nothing at all
except observe those things
as they occur,
is easier said than done,
until you begin to recognize
that you have a conscious mind,
your ordinary thinking mind,
the one you are using right now,
and you have an unconscious mind,

a quiet mind in the background of awareness
that takes care of things for you
while you are doing something else entirely,
it watches the road for you
while you think about things
going on at home,
it keeps you walking down the street,
while you are busy talking to someone else,
about something else,
it does all these things and many more
just for you,
a servant you can trust,
and so you can rest for awhile now
with the full awareness and assurance
that your own unconscious mind
can take care of things for you,
for awhile now,
and all you need to do,
is simply observe those things that happen,
as your unconscious mind
recognizes those things I am saying
and uses the opportunity
to allow you to experience things
that otherwise might be difficult,
just as it takes care of things for you
automatically all the time,
it is taking care of you now,
while I have been talking to you,
it is maintaining you heart rate,
and your blood pressure,
and your breathing rate
without you needing to do anything,
always there taking care of you,
and all you need to know
as you continue letting go
and allowing it
to do those things for you,
all those things that it can do,
while you can drift in and out of a trance
and become ready and willing
to experience something unusual,

something that ordinarily might be difficult
or confusing,
but in a trance can be quite easy,
because you already feel that way anyway
and know those things anyway,
deep down inside,
the way everyone feels
like they are the center of the world,
like everything is about them in some way,
they are the star of the story,
their story,
and so while you relax here
where you really do not need
to even make an effort
to pay close attention
to the sensations in your arms or legs,
you can become aware
that even while sitting there
you can begin to feel
your mind breaking free at times,
extending out beyond arms and legs,
but still aware of the room,
aware of the building,
and able to feel the mind stretching out
exploring the air outside,
touching the trees and grass,
feeling the smooth pavement
and the warmth of the cars,
just a minor exercise
of the imagination,
not even close
to when you really do let go
and allow yourself to recognize
how it feels to be the wind,
how it feels to create the clouds,
how it feels to become the heat of the sun
pressing down on everything,
warming rocks and steel and air,
how it feels to spread out everywhere,
to know everything going on anywhere,
what people are saying,

and what they are doing,
and what they are going to do next,
because it all belongs to you,
the volcanoes beneath the ocean,
the rain on farms and fields,
and able to smother mountains
with blizzards of snow,
able to do all this and more
just by breathing in
and breathing out,
each thought creating something new,
a flower blooms here,
an egg hatches there,
the smell of lilacs drifts through
and wood smoke mingles
with the laughter of children
whenever you think about it,
which you can do just enough
to let you know
how it feels to be in charge
of everything going on everywhere,
being the center of all creation,
master of all there is,
and that is a very difficult thing to do,
to allow that feeling to break on through
into conscious awareness,
to allow the mind to know
that secret held inside so long
that all of this
belongs to you,
and without you
none of it would even be,
because you create it all
with every thought,
or so it seems at first,
but later on now
it may begin to become apparent to you
that all of this today
was just given to you
by some part of you down deep below,
someone you may already know

or already know about
but have not yet met freely,
because that door inside the mind
stays closed most days,
too much power on the other side,
too scary to think about
going inside that far,
going down to back before
you even knew you were you,
and opening the mind
to the possibility
of meeting and touching,
of connecting to
that power within you
that created you,
and everything else too,
the force behind it all,
the energy that powers it all,
the thought that touches it all
and gives you the possibility
of knowing how it feels
to become one with that one,
to be touched by it,
immersed in it,
connected to it,
to feel it flowing in you
in everything you do,
in everything you are,
letting go of you
and letting it be you
in whatever way it wants to do,
allowing you to relax for a change,
to step aside for a while,
while this other side of you
has an opportunity
to guide and direct things for you
effortlessly and automatically,
the way it allows fish to swim a coordinated dance,
and birds to fly in single-minded flocks,
while the lilies of the fields bloom
without a second thought,

and no matter how hard you try
to be in charge of all you do,
it will be so much easier
in the long run
if you simply allow
that natural force,
that natural source of reason
and direction,
that natural source
of an inner connection
to the forces that guide everything,
that part of you that arrived with you
at the very beginning of it all,
a part of the basic understanding,
the built-in knowing,
the universal wiring
that tells you what to do
and does things for you,
makes those perfect movements
and those perfect guesses,
knows exactly what is needed
and does these things and more
when you are quiet enough,
and grateful enough,
and trusting enough
to let it take over
for a while now,
to surrender all control to it
for a while now,
to allow that creative force within,
those forces of nature in you,
to take the reins
and direct things for a while,
while all you need to do
is to sit back and smile
for a while, now,
at the perfection of its ability
and its willingness to just be you,
to do what is right for you,
and for everyone else too,
without reservation

and without consideration
for the niceties of expectations,
which may seem easier now
than it will later on
as the mind tries to drift back
into ordinary patterns
of everyday thought
and ordinary responses
to everyday events,
but if you wish
you can keep that connection open,
and keep letting yourself to be true
because it all belongs to you,
and once you know that there is a you
that is a reflection of all creation
and a continuation of the origin,
then it may be easier and easier,
even as you begin to drift upwards now,
to remain aware in there too,
where that connection is in there,
so you will always be able
to close your eyes
and find it again,
to remember where it is
whenever there is something to do
in the best way for you,
in the best way you can,
whether it is taking tests,
or performing a task,
or understanding something new,
or just being you,
you now know what to do now,
you now know where to go now,
you now know how to allow
that door to open,
and how to ask for what is needed,
and how to stand aside inside
and let it happen for you,
because once you know
even a little bit
about that part of you,

it is always there waiting
to be a chauffeur for you,
to show you want to do
and to help you do it too,
something you know about
that cannot be unknown
even as you begin
to drift up a bit more now,
back up to the surface
of wakeful awareness now,
waking up now
and becoming comfortable knowing
that even as you drift up
that connection in you remains,
a direct line for you,
always there when you need it,
just relax and let it be,
but for now a drifting upwards,
back to the surface of wakeful awareness
where the eyes can begin to open now,
as the mind drifts up quite completely,
more comfortable than before, perhaps,
being here with an unconscious mind,
that long-enduring original mind
that drifts back with you
even as you allow your eyes to open now
and wakeful awareness to return quite comfortably,
comfortably and completely,
automatically holding on to some things,
and letting go of others,
everything carefully organized
and stored away for later on
whenever it might be wanted or needed,
safely available to you,
even with your eyes open,
and the mind fully awake now,
that's right,
wide awake now.
Eyes open,
and wide awake.

Postscript

I may have convinced you in the opening chapters of this book that my primary purpose here is to help people feel better and function more effectively. That is, of course, one of my main motives. As a psychotherapist, I am very interested in discovering new ways of helping people move toward more realistic and comfortable patterns of thought or behavior. Encouraging cosmic, spiritual, or peak states of mind certainly seems to be a dramatic way to accomplish that goal.

On the other hand, I must admit that I also have another, more grandiose and much more selfish motive for my work in this area. More than anything else I want my children, my grandchildren, and their grandchildren to be able to enjoy the joys and pleasures of this world fully and freely. If it turns out that your grandchildren are also able to do that as a result, so much the better.

Unfortunately, the shortsighted, selfish, irrational, superstitious, and violent actions of various people around the world are currently threatening to destroy the quality of our lives, if not our very existence. On the one hand, the entire planet could become enveloped at any moment in the fallout from a nuclear confrontation or a nuclear accident. On the other hand, clashes between religious fundamentalists of various persuasions threaten to send us spiraling into the chaos of perpetual terrorism and a total loss of freedom everywhere.

While all of this is going on we also are rapidly running out of oil, fresh water, and clean air, not to mention the fact that we seem to be busily but inadvertently changing the climate of the entire Earth. No one is quite sure what is going to happen next, but very few of the experts are suggesting that it is going to be good. What they are saying is that bad things are already happening and that matters are going to get worse unless we rapidly do something to change the course of human events. Civilization as we know it may not even make it past the middle of this century if we do not come to our senses quite soon.

Even as I write this I realize that it just sounds like the ravings of yet another paranoid alarmist. I truly hope that is all it is. I have to say, however, that over the years I have seen a lot of people carrying "The End Is Near" signs, but I have never before thought that they might be right. We have been told for decades that we have to rein ourselves in; that we must stop overpopulating, polluting, and destroying the Earth, that we must stop building bigger, better nuclear weapons, and that we must stop becoming more and more dependent on non-renewable resources. We have not paid attention to such admonitions even though they are being issued by people who, whether we like it or not, are better informed and more enlightened than the rest of us and even though their dire predictions are already beginning to come true.

In spite of Bucke's optimistic suggestion (1900) that natural selection is now producing an ever increasing number of human beings capable of experiencing Cosmic Consciousness, we may not have time to wait for evolution (or even genetic engineering) to produce enough enlightened beings to save us from our self-serving actions and our collective commitments to species-destructive superstitious nonsense. If we are going to survive and thrive then we must dramatically increase the number of people who are inherently committed to rational discourse, well-reasoned decisions, and humanitarian responses and we must do so quickly. If we are going to stop the destruction of our natural environment and the slaughter of people everywhere we must begin producing human beings who more fully appreciate the interconnected oneness of all things and, as a result, recognize the obvious need to respect and take care of each other and of our environment as well.

My admittedly grandiose hope is that the hypnotic techniques presented here will help at least a few individuals become more "enlightened", that these individuals will, in turn, help a few others become somewhat more enlightened as well, and that this small change in a few people will eventually help to change our current trajectory. Suddenly realizing, in a direct experiential manner, that everything and everyone is related to you like a sister, connected to you like a hand, completely dependent on you like a newborn baby, and yet capable of destroying you at any moment, can and does tend to change your perspective on reality. It creates a rational reverence and respect for the real world that makes it difficult to stand by and passively watch the corruption and destruction of it all.

I have no idea how many people would have to have such an experience before it would have a significant effect. Probably many, many more than approaches such as those presented in this book could ever provide. On the other hand, I am just not willing to sit back and watch things continue to fall apart without trying to do something. In closing, therefore, let me suggest that now … right now … would be a very good time for you to help yourself and everyone you know enter into a mystical state, not only because it feels good and is good for you, but also because it just might help save the world for my children and for their children's children – and, incidentally, for your children and grandchildren too. In any event, it couldn't hurt.

Meanwhile, I wish you peace.

References

Bahm, A. J. (1958/1969) *Philosophy of the Buddha*. New York: Capricorn Books.

Bownds, M. D. (1999) *The Biology of Mind: Origins and Structures of Mind, Brain, and Consciousness*. Bethesda, MD: Fitzgerald Science Press.

Bucke, R. M. (1900/1974) *Cosmic Consciousness: A Study in the Evolution of the Human Mind*. New York: Causeway Books.

Christensen, C. C. (2005) Preferences for descriptors of hypnosis: A brief communication. *Journal of Clinical and Experimental Hypnosis*, 53, 281–289.

Conway, F., and Siegelman, J. (1995) *Snapping: America's Epidemic of Sudden Personality Change*. New York: Stillpoint Press.

Csikszentmihalyi, M. (1990) *Flow: The Psychology of Optimal Experience*. New York: Harper & Row.

Deikman, A. J. (1969) Deautomatization and the mystic experience. In C. Tart (Ed), *Altered States of Consciousness: A Book of Readings*. New York: John Wiley & Sons, pp. 23–43.

Delbanco, A. and Delbanco, T. (1955) A.A. at the crossroads. *The New Yorker*, March 20, 1995, p. 52.

Erickson, M. H. and Rossi, E. L. (1981) *Experiencing Hypnosis*. New York: Irvington Publishers.

Fodor, J. A. (1983) *The Modularity of the Mind*. Cambridge, MA: The MIT Press.

Gladwell, M. (2005) *Blink: The Power of Thinking Without Thinking*. New York: Little, Brown.

Green, J. P., Barabasz, A. F., Barrett, D., and Montgomery, G. H. (2005) Forging ahead: The 2003 APA Division 30 definition of hypnosis. *Journal of Clinical and Experimental Hypnosis*, 53, 259–264.

Havens, R. A. (1981) Contacting the "unconditioned other": Hypnosis as a mode of communication. *Voices: The Art and Science of Psychotherapy*, 17 (1), 36–40.

Havens, R. A. (1982) Approaching cosmic consciousness via hypnosis. *Journal of Humanistic Psychology*, 22 (1), 105–116.

Havens, R. A. (2003) *The Wisdom of Milton H. Erickson: Volumes 1 & 2 combined*. London, England: Crown House.

Havens, R. A., and Walters, C. (2002) *Hypnotherapy Scripts: A Neo-Ericksonian Approach to Persuasive Healing, Second Edition*. New York: Taylor and Francis, 2nd Edition.

Huxley, A. (1972) Visionary experience. In J. White (Ed), *The Highest State of Consciousness*. Garden City, NY: Anchor, pp. 34–57.

James, W. (1902/1929) *The Varieties of Religious Experience*. New York: Modern Library.

Lutz, A., Greischar, L. L., Rawlings, N. B., Ricard, M., and Davidson, R. J. (2004) Long-term meditators self-induce high-amplitude gamma synchrony during mental practice. *Proceedings of the National Academy of Science*, 101, 46, pp. 16,369–16,373.

Maslow, A. H. (1965) Lessons from peak experiences. In R. Farson (Ed), *Science and Human Affairs*, Palo Alto, CA: Science and Behavior Books, pp. 45–54.

Maslow, A. H. (1970) *Motivation and Personality*. New York: Harper & Row.

Malsow, A. H. (1971) *The Farther Reaches of Human Nature*. New York: Viking.

Maslow, A. (1972) The "core-religious," or "transcendent," experience. In J. White (Ed), *The Highest State of Consciousness*. Garden City, NY: Anchor, pp. 352–364.

Miller, W. R. and C'de Baca, J. (2001) *Quantum Change: When Epiphanies and Sudden Insights Transform Lives*. New York: Guildford Press.

Nash, M. R. (2005) The importance of being earnest when crafting definitions: Science and Scientism are not the same thing. *Journal of Clinical and Experimental Hypnosis*, 53, 265–280.

Ornstein, R. (1972) *The Psychology of Consciousness*, San Francisco: W. H. Freeman and Company.

Prince, M. (1975) *Psychotherapy and Multiple Personality: Selected Essays*. N. G. Hale Jr. (Ed.). Cambridge, MA: Harvard University Press.

Progoff, I. (Trans.) (1957) *The Cloud of Unknowing*. New York: Delta.

Rodger, B. (1965) *Religion and Hypnosis Meet*. Minneapolis MN: American Society of Clinical Hypnosis.

Smith, A. L. and Tart, Charles, C. T. (1998) Cosmic consciousness experience and psychedelic experiences: A first person comparison. *Journal of Consciousness Studies*, 5 (1), pp. 97–107.

Tart, C. T. (Ed) (1969) *Altered States of Consciousness: A Book of Readings*. New York: John Wiley & Sons.

Walters, C. & Havens, R. A. (1993) *Hypnotherapy for Health, Harmony, and Peak Performance: Expanding the Goals of Psychotherapy*. New York: Brunner/Mazel.

White, J. (Ed) (1972) *The Highest State of Consciousness*. Garden City, NY: Anchor.